Contents

Acknowledgements

The author wishes to thank:

John Baird; Liam Belton; Brendan Bowyer; Paddy Brennan (Limerick rock 'n' roll club); Ken Bruen; David Burke, editor of the *Tuam Herald*; Peter Casby; Ronnie Conlon; Midi Corcoran (Tuam Arts Festival); John Coughlan, editor of *Spotlight Magazine*; Dungloe Festival; Johnny Duhan; Roy Esmonde; Ann Fahy; Frank Fahy of Western Pleasure Marquees; Paul Fahy from the Galway Arts Festival; Keith Finnegan from Galway Bay FM; Trish Forde; Tommy Glynn; Mickey Gorman; Maire Holmes; Eithne Hand; Ollie Jennings; Francis Kennedy for his kind permission to reproduce photographs from www.irishshowbands.net; Phil Kennedy; Des Kenny; Tom Kenny; Padraig Long; Joe McCarthy; Fergal Murphy; Kathleen and Chris Mullahy; John Murphy; Judy Murphy; Newcastle Writers' Group; Peter and Ali from Blueprint Express; Sean Potts; Universal Publishing; Ronan Ryan; Heike Schummacher; Renmore Seagull [Michael Duffy, Norbert Sheerin]; Padraig Stephens; Universal Publishers; Declan Varley, editor of the *Galway Advertiser*; John Woodful Studios.

A big thank you also to my sister Loretta for her keyboard skills! I would also like to thank my editor, Adam Brophy, and all the team at Mentor Books, especially Treasa O'Mahony, Kathryn O'Sullivan and that brave man Danny McCarthy!

Dedications

This book is dedicated to the memory of my late brother Francie, who died suddenly in 1998 and to all our musical colleagues who have passed on to the 'Big Band in the Sky'. And to all musicians everywhere!

It is also dedicated to my wife Tess; my son Jim; my daughter Judith; my grandchildren Donal, Bláinead and Seamus; my siblings Marie, Eileen, Loretta and Paddy and my beloved parents – the late Julia and Frank Higgins.

Thank you all for contributing to those wonderful, happy days.

Gor a mhait aguibh go léir!

Introduction

Blowing your own trumpet? Perhaps! However, my musical journey begins in June 1960 when, at the tender age of 14, I started playing trumpet with a local dance band in my home town of Tuam, County Galway.

For the next 40 years or so, I wound my way through the paraffin oil halls of the west of Ireland to the Top Hat in Dun Laoghaire, the Astoria in Manchester, the Lycium in London, the City Centre in New York, the Star Club in Hamburg, the Cork Jazz Festival, the Rose of Tralee and, among others, the Trip to Tipp for the Féile rock festival.

Along the way I crossed paths with such notables as Margaret Barry, Freddie Starr, Chicago's Mayor Daly, Muhammad Ali, Mary Coughlan, Martin O'Connor, Rory Gallagher, The Stunning, The Sawdoctors, Pat Shortt, Foster & Allen and Macnas. I was shortlisted for Alan Parker's film *The Commitments* but failed the age/screen test! It was a crushing blow to the ego.

I played with big bands, small bands, wedding bands, showbands, pick-up bands, jazz bands and even occasionally with pit orchestras for the odd musical.

After years of dancing through Ireland, playing in every parish hall and marquee in the west, having eaten enough ham and tomato sandwiches to kill a horse, I returned to Galway to establish an entertainment agency and music shop and proceeded to lose my shirt. So there I was, at the age of 38, bang in the middle of every musician's nightmare: finding the dreaded day job! For the next fifteen years I worked in the real world with a business equipment company, starting in sales and eventually moving to human resources.

Then, at the turn of the century, with the kids reared, I followed my heart and returned to the entertainment scene. I joined a local station and started a new career as a radio jock with Galway Bay FM, presenting 'Those Were The Days' nostalgia.

My memories and stories of my time on the road are many and varied. I have had the nerve to test some of the stories on the radio listeners and the response, I am glad to say, has been very positive. This encouraged me to keep going and get them into print.

Are Ye the Band? tells the story of life in the music business in Ireland during the Sixties and Seventies, based on the general observations of someone on the inside, a working musician, a musical journeyman.

In July 1960, after a few weeks of casual rehearsing, learning a few tunes, we landed our first gig and things started to get more serious. After that, the ride took on a life of its own, becoming a way of life, a professional career in a world not known to many. I hope that this book provides an opportunity to see this 'world of glamour', warts and all, through the eyes of someone who's been around the block a few times. I also wanted to give an insight into the activities of a travelling band of musicians as a backdrop to the magical world of showbands, a world populated by spoofers and chancers, and the sometimes appalling conditions they became accustomed to, usually on the road.

From the crowd roaring, 'yiz are brutal' to the smell of the van, I wanted to go backstage, into the van and inside the heads of the 'heads'.

I looked at the social aspect of the dancing scene and the huge impact that ballrooms and showbands had on the 'boy meets girl' scenario at that time.

I observed the changing face of the music and entertainment scene, from waltzing through Ireland to quicksteps and foxtrots, rock and roll, the hucklebuck and twisting the night away.

As I put this book together, I wondered about many things. The price you pay for the games you play. The wear and tear of life on the road. The demon women and the lovely drink. The toll of the constant travelling: physically, emotionally and socially. From the excitement of that first night to the hazards and heartaches of showbiz. The uncertainty of never having a proper job, or the luxury of an education or the safety net of a trade.

When most guys were doing their Leaving Certificate, going to college or serving their time at a trade, we jumped onto a bandwagon to tour the world and study at the university of life, on the road in showbandland. Many young musicians, like young footballers, left school in their early teens to follow that dream.

The music game has a remarkable resemblance to the football scene with young lads heading out into the big, bad world, heads full of ambition and dreaming of stardom. Some are lucky enough to become the big fish in the small pool that is Ireland, with a lifespan of ten or twelve years at the top, pulling in big money over a short period. Most, however, suffer the disappointment of never really making it, that sense of rejection, the sinking feeling of not getting onto the top team or into the charts, hearing the words 'don't call us' over and over.

The confusion in thinking you were somebody or something, when in reality you were just like everyone else . . . doing a job, looking for work.

Where Are They Now?

People often ask, 'What happens to old and worn out showband heads?'

Well, I can tell you that they are still there, hanging around, just waiting to be asked about the days on the road. You see, old showband heads never die, they just change their jackets, grow their hair if they still can, if not, get a gig-wig (a sliding-roof) and start all over again.

Some go into management or enter politics. Others re-engineer themselves by changing focus and styles. Still more become publicans, painters, drivers or salesmen. But one thing's for sure, they all love the opportunity to tell you about the time they were in the showband business.

People keep telling me that the big bands are coming back, to which I reply, 'Oh yeah? So is black and white TV.'

Those were the days all right. I was the boy who didn't go to school, but met the scholars on the way home. Well, I too met a lot of guys along the way who were famous, now famous for what exactly . . . well, who cares?

The great or dangerous thing about the business was you really didn't have to be brilliant to get into a band, all you needed was a little talent and a 'lotta thick neck. The more serious the talent, the greater the hindrance. You see, bands were there to provide entertainment, to dance to or put on a show, just like a circus. God forbid you would forget that and start believing your own hype, that you were the best musician in town.

This book is about recalling things that I saw or heard along the way, things that happened to the many, many small-time operators. And remember, there were thousands of us, and after all, we were in the 'business' too.

As Frankie Byrne might say, 'The story you hear today may not be all mine, in fact, some of it could be yours. If so, take a bow.'

Basically, what I'm saying is that any one of a thousand guys could tell this story.

But this is my version.

Are Ye the Band?

One
Beginnings

Sunday 17 July 1960

It's 6pm on Sunday, 17 July 1960. The Angeles bell is ringing and here I am at the front gate with my band jacket on, hair combed, trumpet and music stand by my side, ready, willing and waiting for the van. For the pick-up.

'They said 6 o'clock, so what's keeping them?'

I am watching for the van to turn the corner down at the Tech. My mother said I was the image of Johnny Flynn, the well-known local bandleader. Maybe the fact that I am wearing one of his old band jackets had something to do with it, but I am not sure. You see, he donated a set of his old jackets to this 'new band in town'.

A nice gesture from Johnny. They are a lovely blue with red collar and cuffs. Johnny Flynn is a big name in the music game; he plays in the North, he plays in Dublin and, of course, Ollie Maloney plays trumpet in his band.

'What's keeping the lads? It's half past six and they are not here yet.'

I have a creak in my neck from trying to look around the corner to see the van. When it arrives at my house, it will have to pass by and go up to the corner at Tubberjarlath and turn there. Martin is not able to manoeuvre the van up at Mickey's house, as the road is too narrow. One of the lads then has to run up to Mickey's house and give him a hand with his trombone and accordion, so by the time they get back to my place a good 10 or 15 minutes will have passed.

It's now half past seven and still no sign of the green Austin van, the one that Martin bought from Frank Stockwell, the well-known footballer, who used it for his painting business. At this stage I have my overcoat on and the trumpet is back in the house so I'll have less explaining to do to all the local lads who, by now, have started to move down town, making the big decision on the way down, 'Is it going to be the Mall or the Odeon for the flicks tonight?'

They will all be asking as to why I am not playing after all my talk, showing everybody the advert in the *Tuam Herald*.

What an eejit I feel. In fact, I feel a right eejit!

I'll go up to Mickey in case he has heard anything so that we can at least plan a good excuse for all the wise guys who will be slagging us later on. By 8pm, we reckoned they must have got some other lads, so we are really disappointed and trying hard not to show it of course.

'They could at least have told us, how mean can you get like? And all the wasted hours practicing in Cortoon.'

We decided to go to the pictures in the Mall, so we threw on the overcoats over the band jackets, just in case. Now, it is July, so you can imagine overcoats in July.

'Well feck them anyway, the oul' lousers.'

We headed off down town to the pictures and just as we turned the corner at the Tech, Jesus here comes Martin in a green van with his boot to the floor. He slows down when he spots us, waving frantically.

'Get in quick, we're late,' he shouts.

'Late?' says I. 'And we waiting two and a half hours. What kept ye, what happened?'

'Hurry up and get in, will ye.'

We tear up the road like a bullet, I jump out at the graveyard gate to get my stuff from my house and the lads continue on up to get Mickey's gear. When he's back on board with his gear, they reverse the van back down to Tobin's house. I am watching all this impatiently from my front gate so, as they are moving down, I head across the road, just to be on the right side to jump in for the quick getaway to this big gig in Kilconly, if we ever get there.

'What were you saying, Martin? What kept ye anyway? And where are the rest of the lads?'

'Ah!' says Martin. 'Hadn't we to wait for the priest to finish the evening devotions in the church before we could get the microphones and the PA, so we thought it best to bring the other three lads over to Kilconly to get set up and started before I came to Tuam to collect you lads [the brass section].'

'Oh yeah, good thinking Martin, but it was a pity ye didn't let us know, and we mightn't have cursed half as much on ye.'

You see, we didn't have our own microphones and stuff yet

but, as soon as we had the deposit, we were going to order our equipment from Sean McManus down in Shop Street. Anyway, we were on our way at last, on our way to the first big gig.

'How far is Kilconly?' I ask, as we are belting down Ballygaddy Road, passing Johnny Flynn's and Ollie Maloney's houses, as I'm wondering where they are playing tonight.

'Five miles,' replies Martin in his refined Ballindine accent. I calculate that should take us at least another 30 minutes.

'Have you got your music, Mickey?' I have mine in the case all ready. 'Remember we are starting with "When You And I Were Young, Maggie" and you've got the introduction – it's a slide, a big gliss.'

'Yeah, a big gliss, me and my big mouth.'

Anyway, we're here, we've landed in Kilconly and we pull up alongside the hall. It's a big shed with a galvanised roof.

I'm thinking that it's not a bit like I pictured it. The lads have started playing already and I can hear Tommy on guitar, Mick on the bass and Chris on the drums. The drums are very loud from the outside, the bass drum was the loudest: boom, boom, boom! It is very awkward trying to get through the people dancing while we're bringing in our stuff. There are at least ten couples on the floor.

I better get organised and set up my music stand, warm up the trumpet just like Ollie told me. The trumpet is on loan from Mattie McDonagh in Claremorris.

'Right! Are we ready?' asks Tommy,

'"When You And I Were Young, Maggie" in Dixieland style.'

Chris gives us the count in; Mickey gives the gliss on the trombone, slide – brrrrrrrrr.

Oh no, he hits the top of my music stand with the water key of the trombone and knocks my sheets over.

So here am I, for the first time in my life, trying to play a tune without music, on my very first dance gig. That's timing, definitely a 'panic stations' situation!

It's a very strange, different feeling. There are blue and red lights, people dancing around, people looking at you, the lads looking at you.

Christ, I don't seem to be playing half as well as I did at rehearsals in Cortoon and there would be nobody there. I can definitely sense the live atmosphere, all action, keep going anyway, gammy notes or not, no time for looking around. It's a bit like playing a football match, it's all about what's happening next, like winning the next ball. Hmm, it's exciting, and I like it. Yeah, it's great being in a band. If the lads in the Mall could see me now, blasting it out here, me playing the melody live at Kilconly.

'That's all for now, your next dance please,' Tommy says into the microphone.

'What did he say, what was that about?' I was asking Mickey.

'This time, ladies and gentlemen, we continue dancing with a slow foxtrot and here's Mick to sing "Fraulein" so take your partners please.'

'Hey sonny, does your mother know you're out?' shouts this fella to me.

His mate asks, 'Are ye The Rocky Mountain Seven?'

'We are,' says I.

'Well, how come there are only six of ye in it so?' he quips.

'Ah, one of the lads is sick,' I reply.

'Oh yeah?' says your man, 'Sick of playing with ye, I suppose.'

The night goes by fairly fast and then Tommy announces, 'Your attention please for the national anthem.'

Oh! The pressure is on now big time. Everyone is standing there looking up at us. They all know this one and I am carrying the melody on the trumpet with my lip fairly tired at the end of a night.

So, after Chris gives us two rolls on the drums, I start into it fairly nervously, but then I hear all this singing.

'What's happening?'

'It's the crowd, they all join in.'

My God! This business is full of surprises.

'Well, lads, how was that?'

'Was it ok?'

'Did we go down well, do you think?'

'Were we too loud?'

'Will they bring us back?'

'You were great, you were great.'

'What was I like?'

'Did you think so, huh?'

'I don't know, I thought I often played better myself.'

'I saw them looking at me all right.'

'Well, feck you anyway Mickey, you knocked my stand and you don't even drink.'

'Stall Sham, here comes the hall owner, he's talking to Tommy and Mick.'

Hmm, he's not too sure how The Rocky Mountain Seven went down with the crowd, but they agree to try it all again next Sunday night, same time, same place and he'll pay us then for the two nights, an all-in package deal of £10!

So that's it, time to pack up the gear and head for Tuam and unwind.

As we are wrapping up the wires and gear, the hall owner appears again, walking up the hall with two buckets. He goes to a small window and empties the contents out of the window into a small shed. I'm standing there looking at him with my mouth open and Mick says to me, 'Did you never see a fellow feeding calves before?'

Man, this business sure is full of surprises.

'That's all for now, your next dance please.'

Olympic Stage Show

In 1960 we had transformed from The Rocky Mountain Seven into the Paramount Showband. During Lent in both 1961 and 1962 a big adventure for The Paramount, was to organise a stage show loosely based on 'The McFadden's Road Show'.

Do you remember the old fit-up theatre companies that toured the towns and villages of Ireland in the 1950s and 1960s? They would set up a little tent and do a variety show, perform a two or three act play, a comedy sketch, and various musical and novelty acts like fire-eating, magic and songs. All of these things were concert items as distinct from a dance.

We had an enterprising manager in Martin Donoghue from Ballindine. He came up with the idea that we should tour with a variety show, built around the band, which he called 'The Olympic Stage Show'.

We would hire the local halls, and when I say local I mean within ten miles of Tuam (Cortoon, Barnaderg, Belclare,

Cummer, Ballindine, Milltown and Dunmore) and we would go on the Sunday nights and do this show. It was terrific, great craic. Because of the 'no dancing during Lent' rule at the time, it definitely had to be a concert as distinct from a dance, as the whole idea was conceived to get around the 'Lent rule'. So we put on a variety concert show instead.

It was a seated show built around the seven guys in the band. The main part was a play, maybe a one or two act job.

The first one we did, I remember very well. It was called *The Marriage Plan*. This was a well recognised play which was performed by many amateur theatre companies, so we got the book and we all learned our parts. The guys in the band were joined by three girls: my sister Marie, her friend Gay Meehan and another lady who lived near one of the lads. It was hilarious and one of the lads, Mick Keane, directed it, if that's the correct term.

We spent weeks rehearsing this play, two or three nights a week, out in Cortoon. The format on the night was something along the following lines. We opened with a Country and Western spot where some of the lads would put on cowboy hats and sing a few country numbers. Tommy Ryan was a lovely country singer and he would be the main man. Kevin Eagleton was the MC and he would do some solo singing as well, in the style of Bing Crosby, Andy Williams and Pat Boone. In one part of the evening, the whole band would go on stage and perform numbers like some Dixieland jazz, a big ballad, a little Elvis and a big feature number like 'The Wedding Song'.

The band would do a half-hour spot but in between this and the Country and Western segment, we'd have Willie Brogan. He was a bit of a character who, as well as playing the trombone, could do some comedy. Then we just had to feature a traditional set because Brendan Carney, our sax player, was also a very good fiddler and Martin Donoghue played the accordion. So, we had a little céilí and an old-time band, we had a country band, a comedian, a traditional band and a jazz band, not forgetting Mick Keane doing his seanchaí spot.

He had this story he made up himself: 'In the parish of Glashnameaum there lives an old hermit.' Mick used to dress up with a beard which he made himself, an old tablecloth with hair that he had cut off a donkey stuck to it.

We drafted in friends to do the box office for us as well as other duties such as doormen or stage management. We also had a raffle. One of the big stars of that time was Harry McFadden from 'McFadden's Roadshow' who had a moustache so all of a sudden we all wanted moustaches. We got them by burning a cork and rubbing it across our gibs so all these 14 and 15 year old lads had amazingly dark upper lips.

We also had a skiffle group and I remember playing a tea chest as a double bass. To achieve this you needed a broom handle, a piece of string, the tea chest and away you go, dum, dum, dum, dum. All you needed then was someone on guitar, another on wash-board and drums and, hey presto, that was your skiffle group singing Lonnie Donegan stuff.

I remember the pain of loading up the gear and my sister and the girls making sandwiches for a couple of hours on the Sunday afternoon. Then we would all pile into the van and head off to Belclare which was about five miles out the road. We would leave around 3pm to have time to set up the props and get the whole thing going.

I don't know if we made any money out of it at all by the time we had royalties paid to the writer of the play. The following year, when we looked at the costings of the previous year, we decided we had to have some cutbacks. Mick Keane said he would write his own play to save on the royalties! I remember him scribbling as we practiced away in Cortoon.

We performed this roadshow for two years but during Lent of 1963 we were offered a ten-day tour of England which took the pressure off.

That was our first introduction to the barren period of Lent. There was a story about the resident band from Seapoint at the time, either Des Fretwell or Pete Roxborough, who arranged an audience with Bishop Browne of Galway. A couple of guys went to put their case to him.

What were they supposed to do for the seven weeks of Lent when the Catholic Church wouldn't allow any dancing? Some of them were married with families and they had no work. Well, he just ran them from the door, asking them what kind of Catholics were they?

When you think about it, the might of the crozier and the power of the priest at that time. I wonder what they'd think of the carry on today. Talk about going from one extreme to the other.

Ye're Here, Lads
In the early days, conditions on the roads were rather basic. In fact, at times they could be pretty rough. Just cast your mind back forty years and try to visualise a showband travelling to a gig in a van, seven guys and all the gear. If you were fortunate enough to have a roof rack, you would put some of the gear, the drums

maybe, on the rack. This of course, could possibly make the van top heavy and dangerous when going around bends. If, however, as in most cases, you did not have a roof rack, then you would be forced to put some of the gear inside with the musicians, so you might have a drum on your lap or a trumpet case under your legs. Not too bad if you are only going a few miles, but what if you are heading for Donegal, Dublin, Kerry or Wexford, 150 to 180 miles away? The novelty soon wore off.

At first, The Paramount only played within a radius of about 50 or 60 miles of Tuam, mainly around counties Galway, Mayo and Roscommon. We gradually moved out to places like Scarrif in Clare, Nenagh in Tipperary, Macroom in Cork, Adamstown in Wexford, Dublin and the North.

I will never forget our first trip to Dublin or, to be more precise, to The Top Hat in Dun Laoghaire. Well, like all bright country lads, we headed straight for O'Connell Street, to the Pillar, sure didn't we all know our way from there. Maybe to Croke Park or Barry's Hotel, but Dun Laoghaire? Well now, that was a little bitteen harder!

But hold on! Someone has the bright idea to follow a bus. Yeah, all the way, and we did. When the bus stopped, we stopped. When the bus started, we started. And so it went – stop, start, stop, start – every bus stop between O'Connell Street and Dun Laoghaire with all the traffic going berserk behind us. Jesus! They must have been raging with them stupid culchies in that bleedin' red and black Morris showband van.

We didn't care and we got there in time for the big gig. Up Galway!

A similar incident occurred with some colleagues when on a

trip to London. They did the same trick, following the bus to Ealing or some such 'foreign' outpost. Only this time, the driver of the bus copped on to what was happening and when they reached Ealing, he jumped out of the cab and shouted, 'Ye're here lads. The hall is just round the corner on the left, The Shamrock.'

He was Irish of course.

On another occasion in London when we were not sure of the route to the venue, one of us got into a taxi and the rest followed in the van. There was also a story about a band that toured London by tube, underground that is. Each of the boys would carry a piece of equipment onto the train. I would love to have seen the lads trying to keep the door open with a speaker while they were waiting for the others to come down the escalator with the drums. Can you imagine the sweat, the panic, the mayhem! And the comments from the 'bowler hats brigade', 'All right mate? Hurry up then.'

'Nuff said, over and out!

Doohoma

Doohoma on a cold winter's night reminds me of another time, again in the early 1960s, when the basic services for travelling musicians were very limited indeed. The pre-Supermacs and Mother Hubbard days, when petrol stations closed at 8pm and late night cafés were as scarce as hen's teeth.

The big dancing nights were Sunday, Thursday and Friday, but definitely not on a Saturday except in the cities or in the North. Why not Saturday night dancing? Because the church and clergy said so. We couldn't be out late on a Saturday night because we had to be up for Mass on the Sunday morning. Even in the North, all dances finished before midnight on Saturday and there could be no dancing on the Sabbath. So, you see, whether you were 'left-footed' or 'right-footed' you were caught both ways by the clergy.

Traditionally, the biggest dancing nights of the year included St Stephen's night and, because of the 'no dancing during Lent' rule, Shrove Tuesday, the last dance before Lent, St Patrick's night, the only dance during Lent, and Easter Sunday, the first dance after Lent.

After all that fasting, penance and abstinence during Holy Lent, it was back to the evils of jive, quicksteps, foxtrots, tangos, rumbas and old-time waltzes for another year. Sure we could hardly control ourselves with the excitement.

It was on one of those big nights of dancing, 26 December 1960, when any tin-whistle band worth its salt would have a gig, that The Paramount set out from Tuam to travel to Doohoma Ballroom near Belmullet, in Mayo. The trip was approximately 90 miles and would take about four hours each way, given the state of the roads at the time. So, as usual, when setting out on the trip, we would fill the van up and hit the road, travelling as near as possible to our destination before refuelling for the return journey. Bear in mind of course, that the petrol pumps closed around 8pm in those days.

As a result of the early closing, most bands were forced to carry a spare can of petrol for emergencies, making sure to keep it as close to the backdoor as possible. In other words, as far away as possible from the smokers, which in those days was almost everyone.

When I think about it now, it's a wonder we were not all blown into orbit, or somewhere out there, yeah, the first showband in space! Can you imagine the publicity; we would definitely have got a few gigs out of that.

Anyway, we got to Doohoma, played for over four hours, great crowd, a lot of people home from England for Christmas, then back to Conway's house, the hall owners, for more grub after the dance. Afterwards, it was time to pack the gear and head for Tuam, '90 miles of bad road' to paraphrase Bert Weedon.

We head on back to Ballina, on to Foxford, home of those lovely woollen blankets, oh, how we could use a few of them in the cold van. There were no heated coaches with reclining seats for poor oul' third division, semi-pro bands. The next big town was Balla and, as we were turning left for Claremorris, the bould Martin mentions, 'We seem to be running a bit low on juice.'

'But didn't we fill her up in Ballina on the way up to the gig?'

'Yeah, but we still had to go 20 miles or so to Doohoma. Then the return journey and it's a very windy night and we are "playing against the wind" in the second half, on the way home that is!'

'What about the gallon in the tin, sure that will take us home?'

'Hmm, I had to use that on Christmas Day for the Mass run. The filling stations were closed and I forgot to get the tin refilled since.'

'You eejit ya, what are we going to do if we run out? Let me see the needle, Christ, sure that won't take us to Claremorris.'

'Ah, it might, it might now,' says Martin,

'We'll get some there.'

'It's 4am on Stephen's night, what fool is going to get up and give us petrol?'

'I'll get some from Mattie McDonagh, if he's back from his own gig with The Black Diamond Dance Band.'

Can you imagine calling to see Mattie at 4am?

Sure enough, about four miles out from Claremorris, put, put, put, put, stad, silence.

The engine is silent; the lads are silent and cold and mad. Martin suggests that we get out and push the van. 'Its just a few miles into Claremorris and Mattie is sure to be home by now because he was only down the road in Ballinrobe.'

'Okay, okay, let's start pushing, sure won't it warm us up if nothing else. There is not much point in sitting around here anyway.' 175,866

Jesus Christ, it's nearly 5am, if anyone saw us, big stars and a runaway success! Oh no. The silly phase is starting to kick in, you know the way it happens when you are tired, you'd laugh at anything. Here are six, silly musicians pushing and panting and laughing.

'Are we anywhere near Claremorris yet?'

'Only about three miles to go now.'

'Christ, if we don't hurry up, we will be late for Ballygar tonight.'

Amazingly, not one car came along.

'Are we the only eejits out at this time of the night?'

It seems so.

At last, we're in Claremorris and we free-wheel it in to Mattie McDonagh's house. Great. As well as the band, Mattie deals in electrical gear. Sure the lads know him well. Didn't they borrow the trumpet I'm playing from him because I haven't one of my own yet. It's a nice silver one.

Martin is a great friend of his but we'll soon see how deep this friendship is; a great way to test a friendship, giving him a shout at five in the morning.

'Mattie, Mattie are you awake? It's Tommy here. Martin Donoghue is stuck for petrol. You wouldn't have a spare gallon lying around?'

Or words to that effect.

'Well, God blast you to hell and me only in bed, just after falling asleep, the curse of Christ on ye anyway! The boot of the car is open and there's a can of petrol in it. Take it to hell and get out of me sight,' says Mattie.

Then he goes on, 'Where were ye playing anyway? Did ye have much of a crowd? We had a great night ourselves. Tell me, is that young fellow buying that trumpet or not?'

'Mattie, he's not sure yet but thanks for the petrol anyway.'

'Ah, you wouldn't have a funnel Mattie, would ya?'

'Ara, funnel me arse, will ye get away outta that and don't be annoying me. Make sure you bang down the boot. I don't want the dog to get into the car.'

So, here we are with a lovely can of petrol and no funnel. We're all scratching our heads and scouring around for a makeshift funnel, maybe a bit of cardboard or something, when all of a sudden, 'Hold on,' says the bold Tommy, 'I have it,' and him rooting in his pockets for his clarinet.

You see, Tommy had no case for his clarinet and as a clarinet can be broken into four parts, he had one in each pocket and, sensibly enough, he was looking for its bell.

'I have it.'

And sure enough, he sticks the bell down into the tank and

pours the petrol, glug, glug, glug, a perfect funnel and not a drop spilled. Now I know what they mean when they say, 'Necessity is the mother of invention.' Full well they laughed and all that jazz.

Home James and don't spare the horses, or the petrol either; take a bow Tommy!

Later that night, as Tommy was playing his old clarinet, he turned around to us and said, 'Christ, it never sounded better. I should soak it in petrol more often.'

In the meantime, that'll be all for now, your next dance please.

Two
Have Gig, Will Travel

Carnival Time

When carnival time came around each year, it was like Hollywood had arrived in town for a few weeks. Alongside the carnival of dancing which took place in the marquees, we had swinging boats, bumper cars, pongo and bazaar, all organised by people like Toft's Tower Amusements with their monster raffles where you could win 100 ten bob notes or even a bullock as top prize.

The carnival committee would have their team of unpaid helpers selling tickets at the crossroads and on the buses trying to fool Jim Hand and his band who were on a 60/40 cut of the door.

While the sound of the band was best heard about four fields away, the musicians' experience was that, although a wet canvas improved the sound inside the marquee, the rain might keep the dancers away.

On wet nights, the patrons would avoid dancing around the poles because of rain. Musicians were warned not to touch or rub the canvas as this would cause water to leak or seep through. Some of the committee would loosen the ropes to enable the canvas to sag and hold the water, but then they had to watch for the wiseguys who might punch the canvas to create a splash outside.

The size of the marquees varied between four and six poles depending on the popularity of the venue, with the smaller four-pole version causing major problems for tall drummers as they had to bend their necks to avoid the steep slope of the canvas at the end.

My first experience of playing a marquee was in the parish of Four Roads in County Roscommon around the autumn of 1960. However, I have very fond memories of playing at Hollymount carnival in Mayo on Easter Sunday 1961, because that was the first time I used my beautiful new trumpet, a Besson 'New Creation' with a Rudy Muck mouthpiece for added dynamics. The total cost came to £55, but of course this was paid on the hire purchase scheme, or the 'never never', known around Tuam as a '£1 down and £1 when you catch me'.

The atmosphere of marquee dancing was something special. Where else in the world but in Ireland would you get people to pay money to go into a field, sometimes in muck and rain, to dance in a marquee? Were we mad or happy? Sure we were thrilled!

The Carnival of Dancing

The carnival of dancing was a great set-up altogether with every little village and town getting in on the act. It was a profitable way of raising funds to help local projects that might include the development of the GAA pitch, heating the Parish Hall, or roofing the school. The dancing was usually held in a big, canvas marquee located on the football pitch or some friendly farmer's field on the outskirts of town.

Whenever an idea of a carnival was mooted in an area, one of the first tasks of the community would be to elect a committee. They would meet on cold winter nights to look after all the important work involved in the running of the event. The committee decided on the time of year the carnival would take place and its duration, the booking of the marquee and the bands, and organising publicity.

Normally this committee was comprised of the usual pillars of society in the locality such as the priest, guard, teacher, publican and, of course, the local politician, who was always in the thick of it.

The carnivals were generally run by a combination of representatives from various clubs involved in raising funds for local activities and they would share the 'spoils' equally. Then, attached to the carnivals there would always be festivals, and the carnival would be part of the festival and there would be all sorts of things going on.

You would have fancy dress, a football festival, the picking of the carnival queen, competitions, tug-o'-war, wellington throwing, tractor pulling, all built around the festival and all great fun. When I think back on it now, a lot of them were death traps from a health and safety point of view, but that never seemed to bother us at the time!

The marquee would be situated somewhere near a house to avail of its power supply. Generally, this would mean running a wire out from the house into the marquee. From that would feed a long lead, into which the stage-hands would plug all the bulbs that would run up over the stage. We would have to take the plug off our plug board, replace it with a little two-pin light connector and put that in instead. Sure it was daft as sometimes it wasn't even properly earthed.

The power situation would be ridiculous because very often you would be working on half power. I remember one particular incident in Clare where the place was packed and around midnight, there was a big surge of power. The lights got brighter and the amplifier got louder and started to feed back as we had it to full blast because we were only getting half the power up to then.

As the volume kicked in I asked, 'What the hell is happening?'

One of the guys said, 'Ah, it's midnight so the television is over for the night. They turn off all the sets in the village and we receive a huge surge of power into the supply to the marquee.'

When I think about it, how we weren't all killed I will never know.

As it was a carnival of dancing, the big excitement started when the marquee would arrive, usually two or three days before the opening night. If a carnival was due to start on a Friday, the marquee would arrive on the Tuesday or Wednesday beforehand to allow enough time for the set-up. The erection and fitting of the actual canvas itself was a major ordeal. It was usually the cause of great excitement and fuss with the local lads, as to what was the correct procedure regarding the placing of the poles and the proper tension required on all the ropes. Good weather was crucial, as a wet or windy day would play havoc with the operation and a wet canvas could weigh a ton.

Once everything was in place and opening night had arrived, the local committee would then staff the box office, the mineral bar and control the security. The ladies' toilet might be a little hut, but the gents would consist of no more than a few galvanised sheets and the wide open spaces.

All the marketing and publicity stunts were tried, like putting posters on tar barrels or up on trees. Then you had the big advertisement in the local paper and the guy who would tour the locality with the loud-speaker on top of the car announcing, 'Dancing tonight in the marquee to the music of Larry and the Remoulds.'

Major concessions could include things like 'Hackney drivers free with PSV licence' – provided they could prove that they brought a load of dancers with them. To do this they might have to produce their birth certificates, the size of their shoes and their mother's maiden name before they would get in free.

Another sideshow could be a festival of football. This would be included in a programme of events and maybe, every third night or so, there would be a football match with free dancing tickets as a perk for the visiting teams. The idea being that these big hunks of handsome 'beauts' would be at the dance and all the ladies were supposed to be delighted with this. They would follow in droves in the hope of getting a dance from one of these lovely lads.

Then you'd have things like the tug-o'-war competition, wellington throwing, a sheaf of oats competition, fancy dress, donkey-derby and, in later years, no self-respecting carnival could hope to survive without a Mr Chippy and his greasemobile of a chip-van. Another added luxury might include the presence of a professional photographer to record a great night out.

When the crowd was too big, they would let down the side or the back of the marquee to make space and let some air in. Get them in the front door where they paid and push them right up as far as they could. When it got too packed some people would go out underneath the canvas for a bit of air and sometimes wouldn't be allowed back in. Major 'security' measures usually consisted of a wire fence around the perimeter of the tent in an effort to keep the local dodgers at bay. The odd time that 'security' might be breached, the culprit could expect to be greeted with a boot up the behind from the local sergeant or a vigilant member of the committee.

As payment, the volunteers would enjoy the perks of free admission on certain nights plus a few drinks and sambos. When the carnival was over, the tent would be wrapped and dispatched to its next festival of dancing, which quite often was just a few miles down the road in a neighbouring parish.

And so we were left with our fond memories of happy happenings at the local *mardi gras*. The big bald patch on the village green which lasted for weeks acted as a physical reminder of our wild nights long after the marquee had departed.

I remember a time we went to play at the Castletownbere carnival in Cork. When we enquired on arrival as to where the marquee was, we were told, 'Ah, down at the end of the town.'

So, we kept going and, sure enough, there it was plonked right on the pier. Our big joke was that if anybody wanted to get in for nothing, they would have to swim in from France.

The mention of Castletownbere reminds me of the fact that it is about 40 miles below Bantry which is a fair trip from Galway. I recall the story of one Galway band that travelled down to play in the marquee on a Wednesday night only to be told when they got there, 'Oh God lads, sure ye're not here until next Wednesday.'

They had to drive back home with no fee, bearing in mind the lovely thought of having to repeat the journey the following Wednesday, ouch!

The layout of the marquee was such that on one side of the bandstand was the mineral bar and on the other, generally, you had the ladies' cloakroom.

The facilities for the bands were unreal with no proper changing rooms. You had to get your gear on in the van or at the back of the stage, which sometimes just consisted of a few planks resting on a pile of cement blocks or mineral crates. No toilets so you had fellows using bottles and all kinds of utensils. It was only cat.

Even the skill of changing into your stage wear required some expertise in acrobatics as we developed the knack of dressing while balancing on one leg. You had to take your leg out of one pair of trousers, put it into the leg of another, then into your shoe, before repeating the process again with the other leg. There were various techniques used and, if it was anyway wet, you were slipping in the muck with guys pushing and shoving each other. It was very messy. Sometimes we changed in the van or behind the rows of coats in the ladies' cloakroom, standing on bits of cardboard or on one of the other lads' plastic suit covers.

In the absence of mirrors, there were many grooming techniques used. But the one that I remember as being most unique was the small silver plate on the back of the Fender bass guitar. This would be held up by different guys looking at their reflection in the plate to comb, back-comb or lacquer their hair.

In our neck of the woods during the early 1960s, Con Hynes from Portumna was the main man for marquees, but in the latter days, Frank Fahy of Western Pleasure in Tuam became the new guru. The standard of marquees today is just unbelievable compared to our time. You see them nowadays with chandeliers, refrigerators, hot water and portaloos. Such luxuries were unheard of in our day. We had the bare necessities, and sure it didn't do us a bit of harm!

Sometimes the stage would be mounted on a few Guinness barrels, mineral crates or cement blocks, with no proper place to hang the speakers except on the first pole. Unfortunately this would present its own problems because with the vibration of the dancers, the speaker would eventually start to twist around the pole causing feedback and an imbalance of sound. Very often one of the lads would have to climb the pole and straighten the 'crazy box' speaker. All in the cause of duty!

Powering up the equipment presented many problems because, as I've already explained, very often the supply would come from the house next door. I remember the touring bands, like Emile Forde and the Checkmates, looking on in horror at the way we had to plug in the bare wires with matches, or fix fuses with silver paper. They were the days before the new three-pin plugs with an earth. As a lot of the old halls had only the two-pin system, we often had to remove our own three-pin plugs and push the bare wires into the sockets, holding them in place with matches. Sure it was desperately dangerous, with more than a few hairy moments and the occasional bad accident.

Various Venues

After we had learned the music, the venues became a big part of our lives. It was in them we performed our 'art', the gigs, where the dancing went on. Initially, they were halls, ballrooms and marquees and eventually hotels. Let's just talk about the halls and ballrooms for a while. They came in all sorts of shapes and sizes: the good, the bad and the ugly. But worst of all, the empty.

Parochial halls generally catered for all the parish needs such as drama, meetings, bingo or badminton. So, when a band came to play for a dance, you often found that you had to set-up the band equipment within the set or backdrop of the most recent production by the local drama group, which could be *The Playboy of the Western World* or *Sive*. As the flaps and backdrop of a kitchen scene were usually permanent fixtures, you could also find a line of six or seven chairs spread across the stage to cater for the dance or céilí band.

'Are ye a standing up or sitting down band?' the caretaker would ask when we'd arrive, as he needed to know whether we required chairs or not.

The bigger towns would tend to have new ballrooms but there were a few very creative conversions down along the way. One of the most bizarre ones I came across was in Ballaghaderreen, Roscommon, where part of the old railway station was incorporated into the new ballroom. In the earlier times, I remember often playing in a converted cinema where we'd have to announce the attractions for the following week: 'Dancing here on Friday night to Frankie McBride and The Polka Dots and for your Sunday night entertainment it's Frank Sinatra in *From Here to Eternity*!'

The cinema conversions were great really. A perfect idea when you think about it, because you could just pull out the seats and install a dance-floor and everything else was in place. The screen area became the stage and you had the toilets, the balcony, the mineral bar and, of course, the box office, the all-important box office. Everything was in working order so, in a sense, it was just perfect.

So, 'Good evening everybody as we continue dancing with Don Wayne and the High Noon Showband. A one, two, a one, two, three.' Talk about 'Memories Are Made Of This'.

There were lots of places with no proper power systems, or ones which were not properly earthed. A lot of the halls and ballrooms took years to upgrade from the two-pin to the three-pin plug system. One hall in particular that I remember fondly was in a place called Gorthaganny, a favourite venue of my sister Eileen. It was outside Ballyhaunis but inside the Roscommon border. They had a generator that provided the electric power which did the job grand. As you can imagine, this was kind of unique at that time.

When speaking of Gorthaganny, I'm reminded of a question often asked: 'Where were you when President Kennedy died?' Well, I was playing in Gorthaganny! That dance went ahead despite the shooting. Sometimes, the show must go on.

Then there was the Memorial Hall in Labane, County Galway. That was the Loughnane and Quinn Memorial Hall which had photographs of two guys who were executed during the times of the 'Troubles' on each side of the stage. It was an eerie feeling in a place of entertainment. Of course, the hall was a parochial hall used for lots of things other than dancing: it was a meeting place for the ICA, the GAA, youth clubs, drama groups, and whoever else might need it.

Venues came in every shape and size. I remember in Elphin, County Roscommon, there was this hilarious relief band. We recorded them one night and we used to play the tape on late night journeys home in the wagon to help us shorten the journey. Then one night we recorded ourselves and that soon put an end to our laughing.

In the Cloudland Ballroom in Roosky, The Paramount played support to the George Melley and Mick Mulligan Jazz Band, a big jazz band from England. Tommy Heneghan got up with us that night to make it a seven-piece, using a guitar he made himself. The dance was run by none other than the bould Albert Reynolds.

Dancing the Night Away

In the early 1960s, dancers had a huge amount of choice available to them. Within a 40 to 50 mile radius of Tuam, this being the locality I know best, there was a great selection of venues. In Galway City you had the Seapoint Ballroom, the Hanger, the Corrib Club, the Commercial, the Eagle, with The Talk of the Town coming along in the 1970s. Maybe we are skipping a few years here but Galway always had five or six venues anyway. These would all be public dances as distinct from the private functions like socials and dress dances that were catered for in the hotels.

Moving through north Galway in the direction of Mayo you would have Ballyhaunis, Tooreen, Castlerea, Claremorris, Castlebar and Westport as the main venues. We would then have to mention the smaller towns like Cong and Ballinrobe, along with the likes of Dunmore, Ballindine, Cortoon and Milltown as all of these would have Thursday or Friday night dances on a fairly regular basis. Then, if you headed in the other directions you could go to Loughrea, Ballinasloe, Kiltormer, Portumna and Gort. Also, in the summer, you would have all the carnivals. It was unreal the selection of stuff that you had available and I would have to make a separate list of the marquees to give an idea of the popularity of dancing at that time.

'Up Mayo' – Land of the Thousand Dances

Overall though, the list of venues was unbelievable. In Mayo, for example, there was an incredible amount of halls, even apart from marquees. I often refer to Mayo as the 'Land of the Thousand Dances'.

There were the big ones like Castlebar, Westport, Ballina, Pontoon, Ballyhaunis and Belmullet, and also many other popular venues like Ballinrobe, Bonniconlon, Tourlough, Balla, Ballycastle, Killala and that great favourite, Tooreen, to mention just a few!

They were all over the place and some of these would just operate at seasonal times like Christmas or during the summer. Many left a lot to be desired with no proper facilities. In the very early days some of them had no electricity so you would have to bring in the battery from the car and plug the amplifiers onto it.

There was this famous Vortexan amplifier which was geared for AC/DC. This was around 1960, long before the heavy metal rock group of the same name! AC means alternating current, which worked to power your car, and DC is direct current, which you needed to power electrical equipment. Technical people would understand this.

The big problem was that, having driven to the gig in daylight, your car battery would be well charged, but after you used it to power up the amplifier it would be half-dead. Then, more than likely, you wouldn't be able to kick-start the car, so you'd have to revert to using the starting handle.

Our main worry in trying to get home, after starting the car, would be if the jaded battery could generate enough power to run the lights. On a few occasions we drove on with lights gradually fading until eventually they went out. Then the decision was whether to continue driving in the dark or wait for daylight.

It is also amazing what people would call ballrooms. I remember one, the Daisyland Ballroom in Shraheen. If you saw the state of it! But there were lots of excellent ballrooms like the Royal in Castlebar, Starlight in Westport, Palm Court in Belmullet, and the Eclipse in Ballyhaunis. These fine venues played host to many international stars, among them Tom Jones, Eddie Calvert, Dusty Springfield and many more.

There were numerous others throughout the country like Silver Slipper in Strandhill, Casino in Castlerea, Seapoint in Galway, Oyster in Dromkeen, Premier in Thurles, Arcadia in Cork, the Orpheus and Romanos in Belfast, Capronis in Bangor,

The Top Hat in Dun Laoghaire and the Crystal and Olympic in Dublin.

Some of these were up flights of stairs, like Seapoint in Salthill – three storeys and no lift. I often meant to count the steps, maybe I will yet! There could be 100 steps up and you would have to carry the gear all the way. There was another place in New Cross in London, The Harp, owned by the Byrnes. This place had an unbelievable number of steps and no lift. I believe that about a year after the Seapoint ballroom closed for dancing functions, they did install some sort of a little contraption as there was one spot in the well of the stairs which was perfect for a lift. They just never got round to putting one there in our time.

Facilities

A memorable feature which we experienced when we went to The Top Hat in Dun Laoghaire, the Plaza in Belfast and the Gresham in Holloway Road, London, was the revolving bandstand. Sure it was a great 'yoke' altogether, and there were some hilarious and hairy moments trying to negotiate this contraption.

Where there was a resident band playing, the idea was that the visiting band would get ready backstage and ideally the switchover would happen during a tune. When the resident band was finishing up, they would play an agreed tune and it was ideal if the visiting band could play the same tune. One band would start it, then the stage would go around and the second band would appear taking up the reins. Hey presto, nobody would notice the difference. Oh yeah? Some chance!

You see, sometimes you would have a twelve-piece resident

orchestra playing. You would be expected to pick up the tune with a six-piece showband and hope the dancers wouldn't notice the changeover of bands. Oh really?

The thing we could never get the hang of was the positioning of the gear. You see, it was only the middle section of the stage that would revolve not the whole structure. This meant that you literally would have to pull all the gear onto a little semi-circle and squeeze together until you got around to face the crowd. Then you could push out your PA and equipment properly into position.

It took us a few attempts to get this right. Most bands would put their speakers in position and when the stage would begin to rotate, the speakers would be out on the stationary section. Next thing the leads would snap and all hell would break loose. Then, if you pulled the speakers in onto the little circle, you could not turn up the volume because you would get feedback. There was no such thing as an induction course as to how this contraption worked.

There were some hilarious stories about equipment falling and the stage going around with the drummer left behind on the platform because he had set up on the stationary section outside the revolving platform.

Another time, the keyboard player was left behind, with the 'auld Farfisa' organ. They were a real tractor of a job and when it was cold it was out of tune, so, like a car, it needed to be running for a while to heat up.

There is one great story about a touring band playing at the Gresham in London. As the guys were preparing backstage, the keyboard player was underneath the Farfisa organ getting her revved up for the take-off. He used to hold a hairdryer under the body of the organ to heat it in order to get it up to pitch. But as he was underneath it performing this operation, the stage took off with the MC announcing, 'Ladies and Gentlemen, here they come, direct from Ireland, The Mighty Claddagh Boys.'

And around comes the band with your man down under the organ with his hairdryer. It must have been some sight to watch from the floor.

Some of these situations were not so funny, especially at times when you were up there trying to smile and pretend everything was hunky-dory. You're not sure if the drummer is behind you or if the speakers are coming with you or if the organ player is underneath the keyboard trying to heat her up!

Another case of revolving antics happened in the Lycium Ballroom in the Strand in London, a Mecca Ballroom. You see, a lot of the Irish ballrooms were strictly run by the Irish guys: the Blarney, the Gresham, the Banba, the Shamrock, and the Glacamara.

When the English promoters saw the Irish venues packed, they began to wonder how they could get some of these Irish dancers into their ballrooms. So they started to run some mid-week dances on a Wednesday or Thursday and brought in some Irish bands to play.

The weekends would strictly be Palais bands or English groups. I remember when the Lycium ballroom in London decided they would run a Wednesday night dance and they would have a two-band show. The first band would be an Irish one that was resident in England. The Blue Aces and The Internationals, a band I was involved with, were used a lot. We, the British-based outfits, would play support for the first hour or so before handing over to the visiting Irish band like Dickie Rock and the Miami, Butch Moore and the Capitol Showband, The Pacific or The Johnny Flynn Band.

I was playing there one night with The International. We were the opening act and the visitors were The Victors from Cork featuring Art Supple, Pat McGuigan and a sax player called Chris St Leger. About 15 minutes before we were due to finish, I heard this guy calling me, 'Hey head, excuse me head, does anyone take a size nine shoe?'

He had left his band shoes back in the hotel and the ones he had on were brown. Of course, the stage gear required black shoes. None of his boys had spares so of course, as I was the one with the big feet and did have the required size nine, we arranged that we would swap shoes. Just before our last tune, I went back and stood beside the drummer, took off my shoes and threw them around the back for Chris St Leger to put them on before coming around the other side a few moments later 'doing the steps' in my sweaty shoes.

It's something that sticks in my mind as one of the great advantages and magical workings of the dynamic 'revolving bandstand'.

Parish Hall versus the New 'Las Vegas' Ballroom
When the discos came along you had the one-man disco show and that suited the promoter perfectly: put the place in darkness, add a few 'psychedelic' lights, don't bother painting the place. Many of them were terrible. Some people spent good money and did it properly but the majority of them were low maintenance

with low lights, disco music and low fees. Live music was nearly dead so we started a campaign in the Federation of Musicians called 'Keep Music Live'.

I remember being on the committee at the time and there was this guy who kept quoting the greyhound business slogan, 'Go greyhound racing', so we started this campaign: 'Keep music live – go dancing this weekend'.

But we were up against the advent of the ballad boom, the cabaret lounge, people starting to drink more and it becoming socially acceptable for women to drink. That may sound archaic but it was certainly a factor in the decline of the showbands.

Then, when the bigger halls opened up, they more or less killed off the small parochial halls. This was an awful shame in one sense and it also made it tougher on the lower division bands. It is similar to when a big supermarket opens up in a town; inevitably about four or five local shops close down. It was the exact same with the big ballroom, when one opened up, it mopped up all the dances for 20 miles around.

I can remember looking at old cuttings from the *Tuam Herald* and the *Connaught Tribune* around 1963, when there were dozens of dances going on. They were held in small parish halls on Thursday, Friday or Sunday nights. In one Galway newspaper in 1963, I remember there was a céilí in Cummer, a céilí in Comers in Barnaderg and a céilí in Cortoon. There was a mixture for everybody.

The small halls would operate on a Tuesday, Wednesday, Thursday or Friday night with club dances. But when the bigger halls opened, they would put in a big band on Thursday night like maybe The Miami or The Capitol. The smaller places just couldn't compete with that as all the potential dancing customers within a 30 to 40 mile radius were taken. The main dancing night was Sunday, everybody could dance that night, followed by Friday as at that time there was no Saturday night dancing.

If a big name band came on a Thursday, they would take whatever custom there was in the area mid-week. Maybe only 50 per cent of dancers would go out during the week depending on their financial situation, but if there was a big band venue open they would all go there. This closed down the smaller halls. A lot of the social thing died away with the little parish halls, and also the work for the smaller bands. The bands had to get bigger as a result, and they used all sorts of gimmicks.

The whole culture changed and I think we lost something with the demise of the parochial hall. It was the centre of the small town and would hold one dance a week and maybe a bingo night. The dance could be on a Friday night and the bingo on a Sunday or Tuesday. Aside from dances and bingo, the hall was the major focal point and centre of activity of many a parish where most of the clubs and societies held their meetings and events.

But the dances were a revenue earner that would contribute greatly towards the running costs of this parish facility. When it got to a stage where they were not running regular dances and they had to pay a licence every year, the question had to be asked, 'Is it really worthwhile keeping this venue open now that we are only running half a dozen dances in the year?'

So, eventually, they all closed down. In one sense, the heart of the little town or parish died and unfortunately, in most cases, it hasn't been replaced.

At that time, there were only about 30 or 40 big bands at the top level. Then you had about 400 to 500 other bands in the lower divisions. That's where most of us did our work and with all the business being done in the big halls with the big bands, we found it hard. So, the demise of the parish hall had a profound effect on the middle of the road band and me personally.

The 'mid-week dance' became a threatened species as the working man couldn't go out two or three nights a week. If you only had the big band on one night a week, the average dancer couldn't stay out all night because he had to be at work in the morning.

Also, when the halls were looking for a licence they were faced with a very strong lobby from the publicans, a lot of whom were politicians as well. They didn't want their business taken away so they fought very hard against further licences being handed out. Even when GAA clubs were being set up, they had problems with the publicans so there was definitely political influence being brought to bear.

I should mention that location was also a big factor. In most cases the hall would be located on the outskirts of the town; usually a big barn of a thing, draughty and poorly decorated. When the more comfortable and conveniently located hotels and lounge bars offered an alternative, the hall owners were slow to respond when their patrons were encouraged to visit the various hostelries for the hour or two before a dance. Eventually, the more enterprising lounge bar managers noticed this trend developing and decided to put on bands themselves and keep the customers there. The 'boy meets girl' situation transferred to the lounge bar. With a few drinks in comfortable surroundings, perhaps it was a more civilised atmosphere in which to charm the opposite sex.

I don't know for sure but that's my view on the situation anyway, one of many. Perhaps it was a combination of the lot. 'The times, they are a changing,' sang Bob Dylan. Oh yes, the times certainly were changing.

From the Phoenix in Tuam to the Palladium in Rush, from Gorthaganny, Roscommon, to Semple Stadium for the Féile Festival, venues came in all sorts of different shapes and sizes and I could safely claim to have played in most of them. There were all sorts of venues: halls, ballrooms, marquees, hotels, tennis clubs, pubs, and cabaret clubs. Dances could be organised by the proprietor of a hall, the owner of a ballroom or a committee. In the parish hall you'd have the priest involved and the hall could be rented by various bodies to help promote their activities. Organisations such as gun clubs, garda clubs, the AGS dance for the farmers or theatre festivals. All local associations were catered for, be they the GAA club or committees raising funds for charities and church buildings. There were also agents or promoters who would hire ballrooms and run dances for commercial purposes.

At times the facilities in some venues weren't the greatest. Just like in the marquees you might find yourself without any proper sockets and sometimes, with the variety of plugs, you would have to put in the bare wires with matches. I think it led to many accidents even within well established ballrooms where you could have two separate systems wired up by different 'DIY electricians'.

There were times when you would plug an amplifier into one socket that was earthed and might have something else plugged into another socket that was not, which was highly dangerous. Once, when this was the case, I witnessed a guy catch a microphone stand while holding a guitar, which unfortunately meant that he completed the circuit. As a result he was thrown to the ground, unable to let go until someone succeeded in pulling out one of the plugs.

He told us later that it felt as if he was burning like a rasher and he couldn't understand what was taking us so long to react. But we all thought he was messing. It was only when he fell and banged his lovely Gibson guitar off the ground that we copped on to what was happening. I don't know how he survived.

Another problem we regularly encountered was the lack of proper facilities. Even when the newer halls were built, the first thing inside the door was the cash box. The stage would be at the very end of the hall and off that a storeroom. On the other side, there might be a changing room, the band room, but no sign of a toilet, nothing.

So there you were, up on the stage, and you had to go down the full length of the hall for the toilet. It was desperate really. All sorts of utensils were used for the 'emergencies', bottles, beer cans, sinks, you name it – we used it. Can you imagine the logic of a guy peeing into a beer bottle or can and he after drinking a few pints before a gig, and me trying to explain that seven into four does not go!

And as for the low roofs, when the singer would leap into the air doing his Elvis impersonations. Bang! He could get a nasty wallop on the head.

Lounge Bars, Cabaret and the Babycham Factor

It is generally believed that many of the hall owners made very big money out of the business and put very little back, in the sense that they were slow to re-invest in their premises and didn't follow the culture. The dancers were demanding more salubrious surroundings and this was when the lounge bar and cabaret venue came into vogue.

I suppose one of the major changes that really occurred was when people developed a greater interest in drink, especially when more ladies started to drink in the late 1960s. The night out was now beginning with a few drinks in a lounge bar before moving on to the bigger but sometimes colder, more old fashioned dancehall where the only refreshments on offer were minerals, tea and snack bars.

People now had a choice of entertainment venue. With the development of the cabaret lounge they began enjoying their comforts and so were gradually enticed away from the ballroom. Maybe if the ballroom proprietors had been more tuned in, or were more willing to re-invest, they could have put a case for getting a liquor licence into the halls, but they didn't follow the trends or the tastes of the dancers.

I don't see why they couldn't have put a little cabaret section into the dancehalls, carpeted the floors and installed central heating. People were voting with their feet at that stage. The proprietors tried to blame the bands for not going on stage until 11pm but the crowds were only coming in after the bars closed.

Why were they not coming? Because they were going to the cabaret. It was a case of one blaming the other, a chicken and egg scenario, and the business was lost. I am sure the musicians weren't keen to see it go because it was their livelihood. The hall owners and promoters milked it for what they could get out of it and, as they were generally business people with other interests as well, the decline didn't hit them as hard as it did the musicians.

Anyway, the turning point came when people became more assertive and started to look for more comfortable venues like the hotel and cabaret lounges with bar facilities.

Bar Extensions and Drink Licences

Then came another introduction to the scene, you had to have a licence. You couldn't get an alcoholic drink in the hall so the hotels started to run functions and dances in their premises. Then they put on a light meal to qualify for a bar extension. The famous 'light meal' was a joke really but it allowed them to get an extension. If the public bar was due to close at 11pm, the drink could flow until midnight provided this 'magic meal' to the value of five shillings was provided. That's 33 cent in today's money.

While the patrons could enjoy the comforts of the hotel, unfortunately the same could not be said for the performing musician because in lots of cases there were no proper stages. Generally speaking, the stage facilities for the hotel ballroom or function room would cater for a small group such as a wedding band with three or four musicians, but not for a seven-piece band. So, surprisingly enough, conditions weren't great in the ballroom or function hall of hotels either, but they were definitely warmer.

When the dancers began more and more to follow the drinking routine, the music became incidental, secondary. It became more obvious when the 'disco' was introduced; it really didn't matter who or what provided the music as long as the drink was available and, unfortunately, that was the way the trend developed.

'Keep Music Live!' Who cares? Just keep the drink coming. Goodnight!

Three
Music on the Move

Typical Gig Day

On the road again in those good auld days, pre-Mother Hubbard's, Supermacs, all-night petrol stations, mobile phones, laptops, emails. Oh yeah, those were the days all right, days when there were very few late night cafés or chippers. In fact, up to the early 1970s, most petrol stations closed at around 8pm as they would more than likely be attached to a garage. The idea of a filling station or convenience store was still light years away. Apart from the major towns and cities, the rest of the country closed up before 9pm unless the pumps were attached to a pub when closing times were 10pm on a Sunday and 11.30pm during the week.

The only exception I remember was a place outside Kinnegad where this small English guy had petrol pumps with a small shop attached. This was open all night but you had to buy petrol before he would serve you in the shop: 'no petrol, no sweets' was the rule.

In most cases, the bands worked on a 'one-night stand' basis. This meant travelling home every night after the gig. It is reckoned that at its peak, there were between 600 and 700 bands in the country when you took into account céilí bands, dance bands, showbands and country bands, both professional and semi-professional.

So, let's say the top 30 or 50 were doing good business. That would leave about 650 at various levels, working back through the 'divisions', right down to the relief or support bands where a lot of musicians served their apprenticeships. In general, only the bands in the top bracket could afford to stop over on a regular basis. So, as a result, on the busy nights at the weekend you could have hundreds of bands, big, small, good, bad and ugly, all criss-crossing the country to and from the all-important gig; the one thing they all had in common.

It must have been some sight, all these vans going in different directions like a herd of ants, the common denominator being 'the gig'. I would love to have had a bird's eye view of the set up. I would say there must have been some sights and smells in those vans.

There was nothing unusual about a band working out of Galway playing in Donegal on a Friday night, in Cork on the Saturday and in Dublin on the Sunday. It was quite normal to drive 150 miles, a four to five hour journey, arrive around 8pm, have a bit of grub, put up the gear, play for three or four hours, have a cup of tea, pack the gear and get back into the van for the happy trip homewards, arriving in around 6am. At that stage, roll into 'the scratcher' for six or eight hours, rise around lunchtime, get the Cornflakes into you, chat to the wife and kids for a while, maybe make a few phone calls and then prepare for hitting the road again around 5pm.

It was typical to arrive in a town approximately an hour or two before a gig. You would locate the key holder, get to the venue, set up, test the gear or, as they say nowadays, 'sound check', have a game of indoor football maybe, then the meal for the band at the priest's house or the local café.

If it was a carnival, then very often it was down to the secretary's house for the musician's favourite meal of ham and tomatoes. Nine times out of ten it really was ham and tomatoes. Then some of the lads would adjourn to the bar to have a few pints.

If you started at 9.30pm the first hour might be fairly low key, not too loud; try out a few new numbers before splitting the band for a break an hour later. If there were six or seven in the band, three would play while the others would go for a cup of tea and then they would swap around. The problem was that you couldn't have three brass players on their own, so maybe the trumpet player would do a bit on the bass and the trombone player would get behind the drums for some low-key, simple stuff. Maybe a waltz or foxtrot, something easy to play anyway. Then, after the break, you would cut loose for the next hour or two with all the good stuff, lashing it out, rock and roll and all that jazz. Quicksteps, jiving, twisting, the limbo-rock and the hucklebuck, with spot prizes, ladies' choice and old time waltz competitions as part of the order of the day!

While all this activity was taking place on stage, actions of another kind were underway on the dancefloor.

'Would you like a mineral?' was the chat-up line used at the end of a dance if the guy wanted to test how he was progressing with his current dancing partner. If this was an offer the girl simply couldn't refuse, she would be duly escorted to the mineral bar for some light refreshment.

The culture of that time dictated that refreshments consisted of a mineral bar which sometimes served tea and snacks but definitely no alcoholic drink. All the halls and ballrooms were dry until the dancing scene moved into the hotel and cabaret lounges where, as I mentioned earlier, they could acquire a bar extension by giving a bit of a meal.

Long and Hazardous Journeys

In September 1961, the storm 'Debbie' created havoc throughout the country. From memory, I think it hit on a Friday night and we were to play the following Sunday night at a carnival in Butlersbridge, County Cavan, which is quite near the Fermanagh border.

We left Tuam shortly after midday because we knew the roads could be blocked with fallen trees and the boys brought saws and hatchets with them. I remember going through Castlerea and making three different attempts to get out of the town. The first two roads were blocked but, eventually, we got through. I recall the lads, Kevin Eagleton and Mick Keane from The Paramount in particular, sawing away at the trees. We arrived in Butlersbridge at close to 9pm, just before the dance was about to start. We were absolutely thrilled with ourselves for succeeding in getting there at all, but the committee weren't impressed with our being late and told us to get on the stage and start playing straight away.

They didn't even allow us time to have the meal. Now that would have only taken 15 to 20 minutes but we were told, 'No way, José.'

Clearing Customs in the North

Bands loved going on tour. It was a chance to see new places and have new experiences, but it was also great publicity because going on a tour meant that the band must be doing reasonably okay.

The first type of tour that we would have undertaken from the west of Ireland was a short tour of the North, the six counties, just for three or four days but it was a cause of great excitement.

When going north you had to be organised because, in the 1960s, you had the customs and excise checkpoints at the border. You had to make out a list of instruments and, if you were coming back on the same night, you had to arrange for a time of return. The office closed at midnight and if you wanted to come back after that, say around 3am, you had to tell them in advance and an officer would arrange to meet you there and check you and the instruments back out. If you were late, he would only wait for a short while, so if you missed the arranged time you would have to sit there until the next morning.

One long journey I remember was in 1966 when we went to Scotland for a weekend with The Millionaires. We played in Stranraer on Friday night and Glasgow on Saturday. After that gig we drove back to Stranraer, where we went to bed for a few hours before getting the early ferry back to Larne and then hightailing it the length of the country to where we were playing that Sunday night, Killarney!

On the way home on the ferry we met Prince Vince and the

Kings who were on a similar mission but were playing in Tramore that night. Now, Larne is about 12 or 15 miles north of Belfast and The Kings lads were saying they were not sure of the road back to Belfast. So our driver pipes up, 'Sure I know the road well, follow me and we will get ye into Belfast and won't ye know the way from there?'

Sure enough, we took off and we were belting along and saw a road sign saying 'Belfast 12 miles'. The next sign we saw showed 'Belfast 16 miles'. We had taken a wrong road and were heading north. We pulled into a lay-by to turn around but, as we did, didn't The Kings tear past us trying to catch up to us because weren't we supposed to be showing them the right road to Belfast!

Anyway, we travelled on down to Dublin where The Millionaires had been based since 1965, rushed into the digs to grab some clean shirts and proceeded on our journey to Killarney. The Kings passed us on the Naas Road going berserk because they were convinced that we put them on the wrong road for the craic, just to set them up, but it was a genuine mistake.

Eventually, we reached Killarney at around 8.45pm after changing into our stage suits on the way to speed up things on our arrival. Surprisingly enough, your man wasn't the slightest bit interested in our adventures in Scotland and started giving us the 'what kept ye?' treatment. But at least he did allow us to have a bite to eat.

In The Van
The first bandwagon I ever travelled in was a green Austin van which we bought from one of Galway's famous footballing sons,

Frankie Stockwell, one half of Galway football's 'terrible twins', Sean Purcell being the other half. Frankie had been using it for his painting and decorating business before he sold it on to The Paramount. One of the longest journeys we undertook in the green Austin was a trip to Macroom in Cork. I remember being overtaken by The Royal Showband in their fabulous Mercedes Benz luxury bus and they actually beeped and waved at us; recognition at last. We were really pleased with this 'royal salute' of a different kind.

We travelled merrily around the country in that famous little van for about a year before moving up to a Morris commercial into which we fitted seats and windows. The inside was never panelled so you had all these ragged edges and, with no heater, it was freezing, a real death trap.

We went through Volkswagens, Morrises and Bedfords before graduating, in the 1970s, to the Rolls Royce of bandwagons, the fantastic Ford Transit.

The van had to carry seven or eight people plus equipment, which included drums, PA system, two or three guitars and a keyboard, three brass instruments, a set of suits, hand luggage, marketing material, photos and posters. On one occasion when our manager suspected we were being short-changed by the printer, he got us to count the photos. Sure enough there were only 4,000 when there was supposed to be 5,000, and we never felt the journey to Cork.

For example, The Millionaires showband had a VW minibus with a roofrack and for a while it carried nine people: a driver, manager, six guys and a female vocalist. Even millionaires drove Volkswagens! We had two bench seats in the main body of the van with three guys in each, plus some gear in the boot but most of it went on the roofrack. By fitting the bench seats facing each other you would have more leg room and space for playing cards, but that also meant you had six guys looking into each other's mouths for hundreds of miles!

At times, when conditions were so cold in the van, some guys would bring cardboard boxes to put their feet into in an effort to stay warm. I also knew of one band that carried a Super Ser heater that doubled as a card table.

Pick-up

While working out of Dublin with The Millionaires, the pick-up point varied depending on which part of the country we were heading for. When going north it was Nelson's Pillar, for the west it could be O'Connell Bridge or the Spa Hotel in Lucan. For the south it was via the Naas road, the Star Cinema in Crumlin, where we left a case behind on the footpath one night only to return an hour later to find it still there.

When it was the Star in Crumlin, we sometimes parked the car at the Garda station. We had a lot in common with the boys in blue because at that time most of the force was made up of country lads.

At times, the pick-up could present some major logistical problems. To be in O'Connell Street for a 3pm pick-up would mean catching a 14A bus in Rathmines around 2pm. This would allow us time to nip into the Green Rooster for pork chops or cremated chicken (no Supermacs in those days) before meeting up with the lads at the bridge or the pillar.

However, if one was ever late, it was like the tall tales from schooldays: 'But I was at the pillar,' or, 'I could have sworn you said the GPO,' or, 'Those buses are never on time when you want them!'

As things progressed and the money improved, some bands could afford to have two vans, one for the gear and one for the personnel, but most bands travelled in the all-in-one model. We called it the 'Transit university of life'.

Passing the time during the long hours spent in the back of a van was a major pain and there were many varieties of constructive pastimes. These included sleeping, reading comics like *Beano, Dandy, Topper, Spotlight* or heavy stuff like *The Anglo Celt* or the *Tuam Herald*!

Some guys liked to get in some prep work as we approached gig time. When we would get to within 15 or 20 miles of the venue, one of the lads would produce the sambos his good wife had prepared for him and proceed to have his tea. The idea being that this would save him valuable drinking time while the rest of the band went for the 'meat tea' at the priest's house. Another fella might start to tank up on the concoction he had prepared earlier of cider and poteen or gin, to act as a foundation for the few pints he'd have before the gig.

Rude Awakenings
As The Raindrops passed through Headford one night in 1972, on our way back from Bonniconlon, I was sleeping away in the front passenger seat as usual with Brendan Mulhaire driving. I was rudely awakened by a very loud thump on my side, a car had run into us and then continued across the road and crashed into

a shop! We got out to gather our thoughts and, after checking if everyone was ok, we went across to see if the occupants of the car were all right. We found two girls in a state of shock and very distressed as they explained to us that they had borrowed the car from a friend in Roscommon and were on their way to Shannon Airport to collect someone.

'Hello, but you're in Headford, County Galway.' Talk about being on the wrong road at the wrong time! We had taken a young singer with us that night on a trial run and, as it was his first gig, I was trying to reassure him that life on the road wasn't always this dangerous. After we sorted things out we headed on home, dropped the lads off and arranged the pick-up time for the next night. Surprise, surprise, when the time came for the pick-up we couldn't locate the young singer, not a sight of him anywhere.

We never saw or heard from him again.

Accidents and Tragedies

During our travels over the years we came across some tragic accidents both on the road and in the dancehall. My first such experience occurred in Aughleam Hall near Belmullet in County Mayo in 1961. We had just finished playing and had started to pack up the gear as we prepared to head home. Some people were still hanging around, slow to move out into the night as was normal practice at the end of a dance, when we noticed a bit of a commotion – not a fight, I hasten to add. This occurred down the hall a little bit and someone said that a young man had collapsed. A few lads carried him up to the stage where we pulled across the curtains in order to stop people gawking. They laid

DIXIES

Corks
Dixielanders

Golden Boys
of The Showband Scene

An early Sixties shot of Cork's pride and joy, the dazzling Dixies, with trumpeter John Sheehan in the line-up. After he departed, they continued as a seven piece, without a trumpeter. They always presented an exciting show with handsome front-men, such as Brendan O'Brien and Steve Lynch, and talented musicians, such as Theo Cahill and comedian/drummer Joe McCarthy. A band that believed in publicity, they recorded many hits including Little Arrows, Katie's Kisses and many Buddy Holly songs. On the outskirts of Cork City they had a large hoarding which read, 'Welcome to Cork, the home of the DIXIES'!

The Earl Gill Showband: Included in this line-up were guys who became big names on the showband scene. You had Sean Fagan, Sonny Knowles and Jimmy Dumpleding who had great success with The Pacific. Big Jim Farley had many years of success with his own big band, while trumpeter Earl Gill led his band to greater heights as the Hoedowners, featuring Eurovision star Sean Dunphy.

This pre-showband outfit featured musicians who would later play a big part in the success of the Cadets. They were: guitar player Brendan O'Connell, Noel McCann on bass and Gerry Hayes on piano. Take note of the vocalist seated at the side, a youthful Dickie Rock waiting for his introduction to sing. This was the era when the band was the main attraction with the vocalist as an added extra, e.g. The Tommy Dorsey Orchestra, featuring vocalist Frank Sinatra. In fairness to Dickie, when he got up to sing, he didn't sit down again for about 50 years!

From Mitchelstown in Co Cork, the Maurice Mulcahy Orchestra was based on the style of Glenn Miller and Joe Loss. In the pre-showband days of the Fifties, this style of band was all the go. With five saxophones and three trumpets, they produced a great sound. When Maurice passed away, his brother Joe led the band with great success despite the competition from the showbands. Another band of similar style and popularity was the Mick Delahunty Orchestra from Clonmel.

The Clipper Carlton from Strabane, the band that most people credit as being the first real showband. What a band of entertainers! Great musicians and singers, a band of stars with some great characters thrown in for good measure! Their stage show included a cabaret spot called 'Juke Box Saturday Night', which featured jazz, rock 'n' roll, country and western and comedy. Most new bands modelled their set-up on the Clippers programme and their line-up of trumpet, trombone, sax/clarinet, piano, bass and drums, plus guitar/vocals. Often copied but never equalled. Definitely the original and the best!

Hailing from Tuam, Co Galway, Johnny's band was popular all over the country, especially in the north. They toured the UK and US many times. The photo here shows them taking part in the St. Patrick's Day parade of 1963 in Chicago. The beautiful float of flowers was ravaged by fans as soon as the parade ended. Shortly after returning from this tour, Gerry Cronin, Ollie Moloney and Billy Potter left to form The Ohio Showband. This left Johnny with his brothers Francie and Brendan, drummer Frankie 'Flash' Hannon and trombone player Danny Kelly. He revamped the band and continued to have success with a new line-up, including a huge hit with a recording of the 'Black and Tan Gun' featuring Pat Smyth on vocals.

JOHNNY FLYNN SHOWBAND
Photo taken
Chicago St. Patrick's Day Parade, 1963

Maisie McDaniel & The Fendermen

Maisie McDaniel from Sligo, seen here with The Fendermen, was one of the first female country singers to record commercially. One of her hits was 'Pick Me Up On Your Way Down'. Following a successful run on the TV show Jamboree, which also featured Dermot O'Brien, she joined the Nevada showband. Unfortunately, due to a car accident, her showband career had to be put on hold.

The gimmick of the colourful uniforms was definitely an attention-getter for the Cadets, but apart from that they were a good band who worked hard. Their leader in the early days, Pat Murphy, was an accomplished harmonica player. Their featured vocalist, Eileen Reid, was the first female star of the showband scene. She was a great professional who took her job very seriously and she continued to have success in the entertainment business even after she left the band scene. Eileen married the sax player, Jimmy Day, who was also a featured singer in the band and they were well supported vocally by guitar players Noel McGann and Brendan O' Connell. The other members of this Dublin-based outfit were Paddy Burns on trumpet, Jas Fagan on trombone, Gerry Hayes on piano and Willie Devey on drums. They appeared on TV many times and recorded many hits, one of their biggest being 'I Gave My Wedding Dress Away'.

Taken upstairs at the Crystal Ballroom in Dublin, this shot of the early Capitol features Paul Sweeney on trumpet flanked by the Kelly brothers, Johnny and Des, with guitar. When Paul left to return to his studies, he was replaced by that classy trumpeter Bram McCarthy. Directly behind Des is a youthful Paddy Cole while to his left is one of the first big singing stars of the showband era, the late Butch Moore. Butch really had it all – a good-looking guy with a great voice, a wonderful professional band behind him and he was a really nice guy. He was the first singer to represent Ireland in the Eurovision Song Contest, coming in at a respectable sixth place in Naples in 1965. The other members were Jimmy Hogan on guitar/banjo, Don Long on trombone/vocals and Eamonn Monaghan on piano. With their blue jackets, white slacks and shoes, the Capitol were a class act.

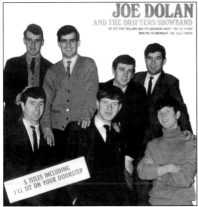

The Drifters were one of the first bands to realise the value of recording. Following on the success of a few singles with Joe Dolan, they decided to release an EP of five tracks. This EP included two original songs by Tommy Swarbrigg who was just beginning his songwriting career. Later on, Tommy and a few of the boys parted company to form The Times. Ben and Joe recruited a new team including Frankie McDonald, Seamus Shannon and Pat Hoey. Working out of Mullingar, both bands enjoyed great success for many years.

The Plattermen were a great live band that always had a strong brass section. I first saw them in the Phoenix Ballroom in Tuam in the early Sixties. The line-up at that time included a young Arty McGlynn on guitar, Brian Coll on country vocals and rock n' roller Sean Hamilton. Playing from 9pm to 1am, they took a break at 11pm and when they returned each guy was wearing a different coloured suit. Towards the late Sixties Brian and Arty took the country route with The Buckaroos while the rest continued on an even heavier 'rocky' road with Rob Strong, John Trotter and Company.

The Royal Blues were based in Claremorris, Co Mayo from where they were managed by the flamboyant Andy Creighton. The 'Blues' were formed when some members of The Pete Browne band decided to strike out on their own. The Gill brothers, Frank and Vincent, Doc Carroll and Brian Carr completed the line-up by inviting four other guys to join them. They were trumpeter Bobby Smyth, guitarist Brendan Arnold, drummer Don Flanagan and singer Shay O'Hara. They were very popular with the Irish in England and the US with their big sound and popular programme mix of pop and country. When they reached number 1 with Old Man Trouble, The Blues were confirmed as being one of the biggest draws in the country and their popularity lasted for many years.

Tuam Brass Band under the direction of Mr Danny Kelly produced some fine players, many of whom later played with leading showbands, orchestras and the Garda and Army bands. This picture was taken after a successful day at the All-Ireland Brass Band Championships which were held in Ballinrobe, Co Mayo in May 1958. The line-up was: (front from left) Mickey Condon, Ronnie Conlon, Christy Kelly, Oliver McCale, Michael Roche, Peter Kelly, Jarlath Canney, Paul O'Grady, Seamus Sweeney, Joe Ivers, (middle) Danny Kelly jnr, Michael Maguire, Martin McGrath, Brendan Reilly, Jarlath Malony, Mickey Donnellon, Sean Madden, (back) Seamus Kelly, Tommy Walsh, Liam Newman, Jimmy Higgins, Danny Kelly (Bandmaster), Jimmy O'Meara, Tommy St. John, Tony Niland.

This is a tribute to the many showband stars who played with bands in Tuam in the 50's, 60's and 70's and who have sadly passed away.

This photo was taken in the square in Tuam during the Seventies showing some of the personnel of four bands in the town at the time. Gerry Cronin and Ohio, Johnny Flynn, Ollie Moloney, The Bandits.

Other bands to have worked out of the town in earlier times included Al O'Dea, Johnny Costelloe, West Coasters, Paramount, Problems, Fleet, Liam Ivory and a Western céilí band. There were a lot of Tuam musicians who were not available for the photograph because they were working with other bands in various places at home and abroad. For example Frankie Carroll, Gerry Mulryan, Gerry Fahy, Frank Fahy, Tommy Walsh, Kevin Kealy, Francie Higgins, Paddy Higgins, Tommy Ward, Kevin Eagleton, Chris Mullahy, Willie Brogan, John Keating, Paul Gormally, Jimmy Geraghty, Pete Creighton Jnr, Mick Keane, Martin McElroy, Padraig Stephens.

TOP HAT

BALLROOM, DUN LAOGHAIRE

IRELAND'S LOVLIEST BALLROOM

FEATURING FIRST-CLASS BANDS, REVOLVING STAGE
NON-STOP MUSIC AND DANCING

THE MANAGEMENT WILL BE PLEASED TO CATER FOR PRIVATE
PARTIES, DANCES, WEDDING RECEPTIONS, FASHION SHOWS, ETC.

UNDER PERSONAL SUPERVISION

FULL PARTICULARS ON REQUEST
WRITE OR PHONE 807155

The Top Hat in Dun Laoghaire was the venue for one of our first gigs in the 'Big Smoke'. As mentioned in the flyer above, it boasted a revolving bandstand and first-class bands, like us! Norman Williams played here for years before moving to The Blarney on Tottenham Court Road in London. So how did a novice showband from Tuam find its way to this prestigious venue? We followed the bus all the way from O'Connell Street!

Premier Aces Showband

Ballintubber - Co. Roscommon

While the Premier Aces had the usual line-up of brass, guitars and drums, a popular feature of their sound was the Hawaiian guitar played by Frank O'Brien. For a band that always did good business, signing English country singer Houston Wells took their popularity up another notch. After their great success during the Sixties, Larry, Andy and Paddy found things a little tougher after Sonny, Jimmy and trumpet 'ace' Johnny Carroll departed to form The Swallows.

The Swingtime Aces from Athenry in Co Galway were a highly respected musical band who had a policy of recruiting and nurturing good musicians. They broke with the traditional brass set-up when they opted for the sax and guitar sound. The line-up pictured above includes (l to r) Billy Curtin, Grant Currer, Billy Carson, Nick McEvoy, Jimmy Reilly and Derek Kennedy. Many fine musicians passed through their ranks including Billy Curtin, Joe Mc Intyre, Joe Bernie (saxophone), bassists Jackie Flavelle and Pat Hoey and also guitarists Jim Gunner and Grant Currer.

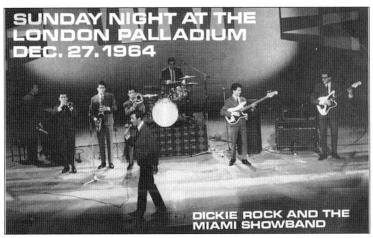

Dickie Rock and The Miami at the London Palladium in 1964.

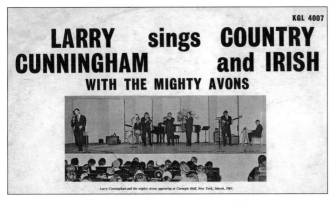

Larry Cunningham with the Mighty Avons at Carnegie Hall in New York City on St. Patrick's Day 1967. They played all the Big Ones!

One of Waterford's greatest exports, apart from its crystal glass, was the wonderful Royal Showband. Most of the boys played with Harry Boland's band before launching out as the Royal. Teaming up with manager T.J. Byrne was of major importance to their success. While they definitely had the talent, T. J. had the vision and skill to develop them into world class entertainers, both at home and abroad!

DANNY PEARSE

TERRY MAHON

ROLY DANIELS

With Compliments of

JIM FARLEY

Bandshow

When Jim Farley left Earl Gill's band to form his own outfit, he gathered together some of the finest musicians and singers in the country. The line-up included vocalists Terry Mahon, Danny Pearce and Tony Woods. Des Moore was on guitar and Joe McIntyre was on trumpet. When Tony, Des and Joe moved on with The Express, Roly Daniels came in on vocals. Years later when 'Ireland was going all country' Big Jim and Roly were together again as Green County. Whenever Roly sang 'Hello Darlin', sure half the women in the place would faint!

The original Paramount line-up in Birmingham on the first night of the first tour of England circa 1962. The crowd were invited on stage for a publicity shot. The man in the 'monkey suit' was the promoter, a Mr McNamara. The line-up of the band was Tommy Ryan, guitar/vocals, Kevin Eagleton, vocals/m.c., Mick Keane, bass, Chris Mullahy, drums, Willie Brogan, trombone, Brendan Carney, sax/clarinet and Jimmy Higgins, trumpet.

Seapoint Ballroom, Salthill, one of the finest venues in the country! No jiving or jitterbugging the notice read! No messing here or 'Chick' and the boys would soon sort you out. No playing in other local venues as all top bands were exclusive to Seapoint. In 1963 when President Kennedy visited Galway, he was brought to Salthill where he was taken through Seapoint to board his helicopter, seen here in the photograph. Notice the Irish and American flags. The banner below the Seapoint sign read 'Seapoint, Salthill, Galway Bay, Welcomes President Kennedy.'

Stepping it out – The Crackaways in full flight doing the famous showband step while the singer tries to cast a spell on us!

The Paramount, with Earl King 'rockin' the joint' at the Astoria in Manchester circa 1963. That's Chris on drums with 'Hank Williams lookalike' Tommy Ryan on the extreme right. The others are, from the left Mick Keane, Liam Barry and Jimmy Reilly (saxophones). Notice the couples jiving, while the two boys sitting on the stage seem to be planning the next move or wondering where it all went wrong!

SATURDAY 26th DECEMBER	SUNDAY 27th DECEMBER

SATURDAY   **26th DECEMBER**

Boxing Night

Dancing 8.30 to 4.30

THE INTERNATIONAL SHOWBAND

DEREK JOYS SHOWBAND
(WATERFORD)

The Tropical Showband

Personal Appearance

KEVIN PRENDERGAST

The Boy from Co. Mayo
Star of Radio, Stage & Telefeis Eireann

SUNDAY   **27th DECEMBER**

Dancing till 3.30 a.m.

Personal Appearance

VAL DOONICAN

plus

THE SENSATIONAL SATELLITES
BELFAST

THE FIESTA SHOWBAND
(DUBLIN)

London Calling

These leaflets/bills advertising the forthcoming attractions were handed out to patrons as they left venues in London. Take note of the hours of dancing at the 32 Club in Harlesden Sat – until 4am! But we got home early on Sunday at 3am. Most of the clubs provided a free bus service to various parts of London to take patrons home late at night. The resident band – The Tropical – featured Galwaymen Paul Gormally on trombone and Lee Lynch on vocals. Roly Daniels sang with them for a while, when Lee spent a spell with the Premier Aces.

Waterford's flamboyant Royal Showband were very conscious of their stage image and always kept up-to-date with the latest instruments and equipment. However when their guitarist Jim Conlon traded in his lovely sunburst Fender for the latest colourful version I'm sure he had no idea how famous his former sunburst would become as it toured the world in the very capable hands of its new owner . . . Rory Gallagher!

Most people in the music business bought the Saturday evening papers for all the latest gossip! Who's gonna make it big this week? Maybe it's our turn? Take note of the advert for the Reynolds' chain of ballrooms.

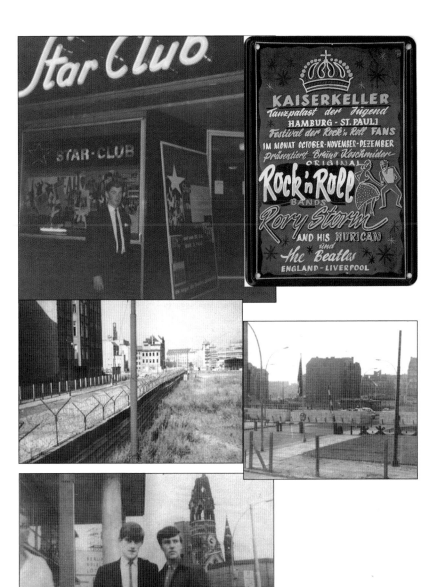

While touring Germany in July/August 1964 we visited Berlin's Checkpoint Charlie, a sad and bleak place. Thankfully it is no longer needed to keep the city divided. The top left photo shows Chris outside the Star Club in Hamburg, a popular spot for touring British groups. The Beatles played there circa 1961 and 1962. The International Showband played there during the summer of 1964. The bottom left photo shows Jimmy Higgins and Frankie Dwyer in Berlin with the partly bombed cathedral in the background.

A stylish Miami with their classy suits, shiny instruments and luxury bus. These boys were treated like royalty with all the comforts laid on compared to the rest of us. But we didn't complain because we were hoping to be the next 'big thing'. Our big break could be just around the corner.

'It's a long way to Tipperary' according to the song, but I'm sure that never bothered 'Kevin Flynn and the Editors' as they toured around Ireland travelling to and from the gigs in their sturdy old bandwagon. Unfortunately not everyone enjoyed such comfort!

MUSIC ON THE MOVE

him on the stage and he died almost immediately. He was only 19 years of age and, as I was only 15 at the time, this was a very daunting experience.

Some months later, while on tour in England, we were travelling from Manchester to Leeds and had crossed the Pennines. Due to a traffic accident, there was a delay on the road and word filtered back that someone had been run over. As the traffic moved off, we were all stretching our necks to get a look at the casualty victim and, when we eventually saw the poor unfortunate man just thrown there on the road, my stomach turned with the most sickening feeling that I ever experienced. Of course, just like everyone else I had to have a good look so it served me right.

My next horrific encounter with death on the road was in Mountbellew, County Galway, in the early 1970s. On leaving the town to return home to Galway City after playing in the marquee, there was a hold up in traffic just a few miles out the road. A pedestrian was hit by a car and knocked into the ditch and was killed outright. A local guard was at the scene along with the doctor and his wife and of course a crowd of onlookers which now included a few of the band. As the poor man was already dead, a request for an ambulance from Ballinasloe was declined. This was normal practice, I was told, when the victim was already dead.

So, the plan was to take the body to Ballinasloe Hospital in the doctor's car. Now the doctor's wife asked for assistance to lift the body out of the ditch and to my amazement, people started to shuffle away. Out of embarrassment, a few of us volunteered to lift the body out and into the car. Vinny lifted him by the

61

shoulders with Brendan and me on either side lifting each leg. As soon as we lifted him there was a groan with the release of air. What a fright we got, especially poor Vinny who was closest to the head. An experience I will never forget and one I would not like to repeat.

Many years later, while playing for a corporate function in the Corrib Great Southern Hotel, Galway, I witnessed another tragic event. The procedure was a typical conference format; national delegates attend an AGM during the day, and then relax in their rooms for a few hours before dinner at eight. The meal and speeches would be completed well before midnight, and then dancing until two.

As usual, when the formalities were over some people drifted into the bar while some others loved to dance. We were less than an hour into the dancing – jiving and waltzing, they were of that age group, forties and fifties, – when this man who we had noticed was a very good jiver, collapsed and fell to the floor. He started to turn blue and died almost immediately. We stopped the music straight away and an eerie silence descended on the place. We asked the patrons to leave the room and most of them did except for a few of the man's friends. The ambulance was called and it arrived within minutes. They wheeled him away and that was that. You just couldn't believe how suddenly the whole thing happened, about 30 minutes all told. Worst of all, as it was a 'delegates only' conference, meaning there were no partners, his friends had to ring his poor wife in Dublin and tell her the story. I certainly felt for them.

With so many bands travelling so many miles over so many years, it was inevitable that some tragedies would occur. Some of our colleagues who were involved in crashes going to and from gigs included: Maisie McDaniels, Sheeba, Tina and The Real McCoy. These were the lucky ones who survived; however, there were many who unfortunately did not.

People like the late Tom Dunphy, Tommy Ryan, Billy Kelly, Big Ivan, Paul Williams, Tony Walsh and Dermot Woodfull. It was terribly sad that so many should lose their lives going to or coming from work. Spare a thought also for the six people (including four brothers) who lost their lives in the terrible crash involving The Statesiders from Derry. Of course, we will never forget the three young men, Fran O'Toole, Brian McCoy and Tony Geraghty, who were gunned down near Newry in the terrible 'Miami Massacre'. May God be good to them all.

Intercontinental Transport Problems
Trains to Philadelphia, Here We Come!

During one of our American trips, The Millionaires had to travel from New York to Philadelphia by train and, as was often the case, we were very tight for time. So, as Johnny and I went to get the tickets, the rest of the boys were instructed to get onto the train with the luggage and equipment. However, time must have been tighter than we imagined because the train took off before we arrived back with the tickets. So, here you had the six guys with all the gear travelling merrily along their way to Philadelphia with no tickets and them sweating blood in case they'd be put off at some place along the way. They didn't panic too much at first as they thought that Johnny and I would have jumped onto a carriage further up the train. But, as time and the train moved on and we weren't appearing, it was dawning on them that we mustn't have made it, so they were on their own. With all the talk and fuss that must have been going on, the other passengers soon copped on to the lads' dilemma and began to join in the adventure, 'Hey man, I just can't wait to see what happens to you guys with all this gear and no tickets.'

Johnny and I had to catch the next train out which was only about 40 minutes later. However the guys travelled right into the Central Station while we got off at the first stop in Philly, just in case the boys had done the same! So, we had to wait another 40 minutes for the next train and eventually arrived into Central Station where we received a 'wonderful reception' from the boys.

On a trip from Victoria Station in London to Manchester, again cutting it rather tight for time, we had the inevitable panic in trying to get all the gear on to the train. As we all hurried along with different pieces of equipment, Pat 'Onions' Green was running along the platform with a case full of shoes, which contained seven pairs of black and seven pairs of brown.

Guess what happened? You're right!

The clips on the case slipped open and all the shoes spilled out all over the platform causing mayhem and major panic. Can you imagine the punctual passengers sitting on the train watching this entire circus unfold? Nevertheless, we did succeed in recovering the lot just in time to catch the train.

Rent-A-Crowd

On a visit to Kiel during our German tour of 1964, the local promoter decided to pull off a rent-a-crowd stunt in an effort to get some publicity, so he took us down to the local train station. There, as people alighted from a train we mingled with the passengers, and he had arranged for a group of screaming girls to run towards us looking for autographs while some photographers took shots as we were 'mobbed' by fans! He even succeeded in having some of the pictures published in the local press.

Trusty Old Tractor

The modes of transport used were many and varied in the often valiant efforts made to get to the gig at all costs. In Ireland, the trusty old tractor was called into action on many an occasion to pull us out of a ditch. There was a dangerous 'S' bend between Claremorris and Ballindine which claimed a few victims in its time. It also resulted in being a bit of a nuisance for the local farmers who were called on at some unearthly hours to give a hand and to get us back on the road again.

Via Brooklyn Bridge, Harlem

On one of our illustrious trips to New York we were met at the airport by the promoter, a Leitrim man by the name of Bill Hartigan who worked in the construction trade for the day job. This seemed to be quite a common trend on the Irish scene abroad, builder by day and dance promoter by night.

When Bill came to meet us at the airport he arrived in his pick-up truck, open back and all. We, of course, being full of high spirits having just arrived in the 'city that never sleeps' thought this was great craic, so while two of the guys got in the front with Bill, the rest of us hopped in the open back with all the gear.

We headed for the city and pretty soon the novelty started to wear thin on this great adventure over Brooklyn Bridge in the open air. Every time we stopped at traffic lights one of the guys would jump from the back to try and squeeze into the cab with Bill and the boys to avoid freezing to death in the back of the truck.

Along the way, Bill remembered he needed some electrical equipment so he pulled in somewhere in Harlem and disappeared into a hardware store to do some shopping, leaving the 'brass monkeys' minding the truck. Of course we were approached by a few unfortunates looking for a handout but, despite our high pitched Irish voices, they seemed to get the message and took off.

Of course, we vowed never to tell the story of the pick-up truck on Brooklyn Bridge to anybody, especially fellow musicians, so as not to spoil the myth of us being huge stars in New York.

Some time later, while talking to some friends from The Casino Showband, who were later to become The Indians, I let it slip about the transport arrangements from New York airport and they quickly looked at each other before bursting into laughter. They too had been on the receiving end of Big Bad Bill's pick-up truck at the airport and, like ourselves, didn't dare tell anyone.

Afterwards, we wondered if this was a big prank that Bill played on all the starstruck greenhorns from showband land?

When travelling to England on our first trip we drove the van to the North Wall in Dublin where it was strapped onto a contraption and then lifted by crane onto the boat. The scary part was that our driver, Martin Donoghue, remained in the driver's seat during the procedure.

We had some weird and wonderful experiences in our efforts to get to various gigs. When playing for a Saturday dance at the

Corrib Rowing Club in Galway, arrangements had to be made to take the van through the nearby IMI factory. On the odd occasion when the keyholder couldn't be located, we had to park the van on the main road, load the equipment into a small boat and row the gear up river to the club.

And Planes

On another occasion, while travelling from Dublin to Belfast on a busy Friday evening, our drummer Mike O'Brien, who was a trainee pilot, decided to add to his flying hours by taking a four seater to Aldergrove airport. He didn't have any great difficulty in convincing Joe Doherty and myself to travel as 'co-pilots'.

And Food

'Where do we get the meal, lads?'

'Up at the priest's house, the finest meal ye ever clapped an eye on, the meat tea at the priest's house.'

Smiths for the chips, Harry's for the works, and the Night Bite for the half sausage sandwich.

We must have had ham and tomatoes at every crossroads in Ireland, so whatever you do, never ever offer ham and tomatoes to a musician. You will lose a friend.

We must have eaten everywhere, from crubeens in Headford to tea and sandwiches from a tin box in Mayo, soup in Kilkenny and 'grass' sandwiches in Cork.

What about the band that ate the 'bones' in the Chinese restaurant in Dublin? Or the Wimpy and the Golden Egg at the Marble Arch in London, or the nice neat little diamond sambos you would get in the North? You would get beans on toast in

Donegal, one slice each, while that would be a 'thousand guys on a raft' in New York. But a rasher? 'Hey man, what's a "rasher"?'

You could relish a steak and kidney pie in Birmingham or a raw meat breakfast in Kiel in Germany. Also, you could avail of the vol-au-vents and pommes frites in the Mambo Shankey in Hamburg. Or, again in New York, you could get all you could eat for five dollars.

'Could I have four T-bone steaks, please?'

'No, sorry sir, you got to get soup first, then there is the main meal, the dessert and the coffee. Then you can come back and we'll give you the same again, as many times as you like!'

Or then again, you could call to the Treaty Café in Limerick for a 'furry' burger or, if you were in Dublin, you could call to Gig's Place or Joe's Steakhouse or Molly's, before you go to the Night Bite on the quays on the way home.

'Could I have half a sausage sandwich, please?'

'And who'll have the other half?'

But hurry because your chips are going cold in Macroom.

Goslo

One snowy night, we were returning home from a gig and approaching a small town. The driver, who wasn't quite sure where we were, couldn't make out the name of the place as the sign was partially covered with snow.

'Where are we now?' he enquired wearily, to anyone who might be awake.

'Ah, Goslo, I think,' replied the sleepy co-pilot.

'Goslo,' sighed the driver, 'Sure there's no such place as Goslo.'

And with that he stopped the van, jumped out and went over and wiped the snow off the sign, which read: 'Go Slow'.

Richie

During one of our never-ending tours entertaining the Irish emigrants abroad, we arrived in Birmingham and after we located the venue, I dropped the boys and equipment off to get set up. Meanwhile, I headed on down to the Coventry Road area to organise some accommodation in one of the small B&B joints that we used to frequent.

I rang the doorbell and as I was explaining to the young lady who answered that we were an Irish band on tour looking for digs for the night, I noticed a woman at the top of the stairs.

'Are ye Richie Gallagher?' she shouted down to me in a concerned voice. I assured her that we most definitely were not Richie Gallagher so she said, 'Ok, ye can come in so.'

Obviously, Richie and the boys must have been acting the maggot on a recent visit and were giving us all a bad name! We didn't need any help in that department as we were well capable of achieving that accolade under our own steam.

Any Waste Porter, Lads?

This was the enquiry by a local character in Kilkishen marquee in County Clare as the boys were guzzling down a few well-deserved bottles of Guinness behind the stage. He had done fierce minding on us all night, bringing us drinks from the mineral bar and stopping people from sitting on the stage, all that sort of thing. We had just finished a three to four hour session playing for well over 1,000 people on the opening night of Kilkishen

Carnival on Easter Sunday, 1969, where our fee for the night was in the region of £130.

Having just returned from a three week tour of the States where we were treated like lords, we were having difficulty in getting back to reality. I mean, 'Hey man, how can we raise our speakers off the ground and elevate them on to the pole?'

'Ah, with a bitteen of rope I suppose.'

'And can you get me a coke from the cooler?'

'Ah, what's a cooler?'

What Do We Play at the End?

Because of the political situation in the North, you always had to be sensitive when playing in the various halls. There were Protestant halls, Catholic halls and mixed halls. One of the first questions you would always ask when you arrived at a new venue was if you should play anything at the end of the night. In one place you would play *God Save The Queen*, in another you would play *Amhrán na bhFiann*, while in yet another, you wouldn't play anything at all or you could be asked to play *Faith of our Fathers*.

I had a bit of a raw experience on one occasion. I remember asking the security man, 'Do we play anything at the end?'

To which he replied, 'Yes.'

I then had to ask, 'What do we play?'

He said, 'The anthem.'

I, of course, had to ask, 'Which one?'

And he replied, 'There's only one.'

'Is it *The Queen*?'

'Well, what do you think?' he answered.

The story is told about a band from Monaghan that played in Capronis in Bangor on a Saturday night. You had to stop playing before midnight because there was no dancing on the Sabbath. They had a notice up in the band room informing the musicians to play *The Queen* at quarter to twelve.

So, it was this band's first time playing that venue and, at the appointed time, the drummer 'rolled in' the anthem. While half the band started playing *The Soldier's Song*, the other half started into *The Queen* and there was absolute mayhem. Your heart would go out to the boys, just imagine the embarrassment and panic.

The Changing Times of the Sixties
Good times beginning,
On the up,
We were winning,
With Kennedy in the White House,
And Lemass in Leinster House,
Bowyer sang the 'Hucklebuck',
It was top of the charts,
While The Beatles at the Palace
Collected 'purple' hearts,
Bobby Moore was leading England
To World Cup glory,
While Galway's three-in-a-row
Was quite another story.

With the IDA providing factories and jobs,
Most people were earning a nice few bob,
We had marquees, ballrooms and Swingtime Aces,
All putting smiles on peoples faces,
Mini-skirts and Mini cars,
Mohair suits and lounge bars,
Showbands were singing,
Dancers were swinging,
Yeah, everyone's rocking and rolling!
So! Roll over Beethhoven,
'Cos here comes Joe Dolan!

Four
Come Follow The Band

Are Ye a Standing Up or a Sitting Down Band?

During the pre-showband days of the late Fifties, between 1956 and 1959, the musical entertainment for dancers was provided by dance bands, orchestras and céilí bands. The most popular céilí bands would have included: The Gallowglass, Donal Ring (Cork), Johnny Pickering, Richie Fitzgerald (Bundoran), Jackie Hearst, the Tulla and Kilfenora from Clare. Galway provided the likes of Kilimor, Kiltormer, Aughrim Slopes, and Mulhaires to name but a few.

The late 1950s was also the era of the dance band, in the style of Joe Loss and Glenn Miller. Strict tempo for ballroom dancing was provided by such household names as Des Fretwell, Chick Smyth, Des Furlong, Chris Lamb, Earl Gill, Brose Walsh, Jack Ruane, Stephan Garvey, Bert Flynn, Jimmy Wiley, Dave Dixon, Jack Barrett, Hughie Trainer, Donie Collins, Maurice Mulcahy, Mick Delahunty, and Tommy O'Brien who led the resident band in the Crystal in Dublin.

In the Seapoint ballroom, Salthill, Galway, The Des Fretwell Orchestra was the resident band with visiting bands coming in on Thursdays and Sundays. If you went there on a Thursday in the early 1960s, you would see Des Fretwell with his orchestra, led by Gerry Macken, sitting down, reading and playing the dance music. Then, at 11pm, the showband would arrive on stage in their flashy suits, jumping around the place, with no music stands, playing pop music – all the top chart hits from the UK and the US. When someone later described a showband as being akin to a live jukebox, it wasn't a bad description.

The arrival of the 1960s heralded the launch in earnest of a wave of new, all-singing, all-dancing showbands with their glitzy multi-coloured suits, fancy steps and glamorous names. Some of the venues borrowed names from the exotic world of Hollywood. Before long, the entertainment world of Ireland was dazzled with names like: Las Vegas, Waldorf, Adelphi, Ritz, Carlton, Astoria, Carousel, Embassy, Paramount, Top Rank, and Dreamland.

When launching a new showband, the managers were just as flamboyant. A major part of the deal was having a flashy, punchy, catchy name like: The Royal, Capitol, Miami, Pacific, Caroline, Savoy, Casino, Embassy, Graduates, Chessmen, Freshmen, or Plattermen. Some bands called themselves after internationally famous ballrooms and cinemas like Mayfair or Savoy, and The Miami became trendsetters by choosing the name of an American state. So began a bit of a run on names like: Pacific, Ohio, Sante Fe, Sahara, Oklahoma, Sands.

We also had Altonaires, Clefonaires, Debonaires and Millionaires. Mellowchords, Airchords, Royal Chords and Discords. Black Aces, Blue Aces, Premier Aces and Swingtime Aces.

Of course, it was another way of distinguishing the different styles between a dance band or orchestra and the new trendy, all-singing, all-dancing showband.

Naming a Band

Back in the late Fifties, most bands were called after the owner or leader, for example Johnny Flynn, Johnny Quigley, and Gay McIntyre. Jack Brierley from Cork, Kevin Flynn and Jack Hanly from Tipperary, Hughie Traynor from Armagh, Donie Collins, Maurice Mulcahy and Mick Delahunty. There was Brose Walsh from Castlebar, Jack Ruane from Ballina, Sid Shine from Athlone, Kevin Woods, Michael O'Callaghan, Chick Smyth, Chris Lamb, Jimmy Crompton from Belfast and Jimmy Wiley from Tipperary.

There was a great story about Jimmy Wiley. When the phone would ring he'd shout, 'Don't answer that phone; it could be somebody trying to cancel another gig.'

Initially, some of the old style dance bands resisted the change but eventually they did re-adjust their approach and traded in their tuxedos for blue mohair suits, dispensed with their seats and music stands and joined the mass of moving musicians doing the steps.

Showbands

Ollie Maloney, a well known character of the time, recalls two of the major changes that assisted the transformation from orchestra to showband. These were standing up while playing and getting a manager.

Just to give it some sort of a handle, a point I would like to make here is that showbands, from my reckoning, were very much a nationwide thing. They came from all over the country. It wasn't just a case of Dublin and other major cities leading the way. By that I mean, from the late 1950s and right up to 1964, the scene mainly involved a couple of local fellows starting a band, like The Clipper Carlton did. They were a dance band from Strabane. The Royal Showband was formed by a couple of local lads deciding to have a go in Waterford. Johnny Flynn had a dance band in Tuam.

The trend at that time was that the leader would own the band, in other words he owned the van, equipment, and suits, and he would pay the lads per night. From Cork came The Regal and The Dixielanders (Dixies). Donie Collins had a band in Limerick and the Dolan brothers started The Drifters in Mullingar.

You will note at this stage that it was mainly rural bands. There were hundreds of them with very few coming from the major cities, Derry and Cork being the noted exceptions.

Probably the first showband from the city of Dublin to make an impact nationally would have been The Cadets. The members were all from Dublin but they were led by Pat Murphy and managed by Tom Costello who was from Mayo. He happened to be the manager of the Crystal Ballroom so he saw the trend developing. The rural bands were coming and playing in his venue and from talking to the likes of Johnny Flynn, he could see there was a market there for a band that would play a good mixture of the top 20 pop hits and country and western. With their classy uniforms and superb female vocalist in Eileen Reid,

The Cadets made a huge impact on the scene and people still remember them as being one of the top showbands of that time.

The Capitol Showband

Another major force to emerge around that time was a band that would challenge The Royal for the number one spot, The Capitol. They were led by Galwayman, Des Kelly, who already had a band in Galway called The Quicksilver.

When Des went to college in Dublin he soon saw the potential for bigger things, so with his brother Johnny on drums and two guys from Donegal, trumpeter Paul Sweeney and pianist Eamon Monaghan, along with two from Dublin, Butch Moore and Jimmy Hogan, and finally with Paddy Cole of Monaghan and a Corkman, Don Long, he founded what was to become one of the most polished outfits of the entertainment circuit.

These Capitol guys were groomed and modelled to create a sound that was, in my opinion, a cross between The Clipper Carlton and The Royal. They were hand picked and went on to become one of the first of what could be called the 'designer' or 'purpose built' bands. They were very professional, all good musicians and singers, well rehearsed, wore lovely suits, and everything about them was class.

Then, after The Capitol and The Cadets, came The Miami with Dickie Rock as lead vocalist, and The Pacific, featuring Sean Fagan and Sonny Knowles. These were the first out and out Dublin bands. The Miami were a pop band and didn't play country music, whereas The Cadets, like most of the bands, would play a mixture. When it came to the stage where the musicians were being hand picked, then obviously the bands were becoming more professional and slick all the time. But somehow, they didn't seem to have this raw magic that The Royal and The Johnny Flynn Band had, and it's interesting to note that both of these bands were among the biggest and most successful to play the North. While they may not have been the classiest musicians, they certainly had this very definite unique sound and, entertainment wise, they had a lot to offer.

At this stage also, managers and agencies started to command a bit more power within the business. This, in time, would result in making things more difficult on the individual guy trying to start up his own band and work off his own bat. You had to get a manager with good connections or become affiliated to some agency or other. It was becoming more political and things got tougher for the small solo operator.

Regional Bands

Each region had its own special bands and, while they might be very popular locally, some of them would rarely move out of their province and sometimes not even beyond two or three counties. In Munster, I am thinking in particular of The Michael O'Callaghan Band from Buttevant, north Cork. Michael O'Callaghan was very big in the Munster region, and he had been doing four to five nights a week within an 80 to 100 mile radius of home for years, although later he started to go nationwide.

Other regions had similar situations. In Mayo, you would have Brose Walsh, who played mostly just along the west coast but would also play in Dublin for specialist work such as adult dancing. This was a different scene as there was always a kind of adult dance set up and while they would only usually play in their own regions, they would occasionally go to Dublin for weekends. But they always played plenty of private functions like Hunt Balls and this helped fill their diary for many years even after the ballroom days finished.

The North was another case in point. There were quite a few bands up there who rarely came south and some southern bands that never went north.

Just a few off the top of my head would be The Jimmy Johnston Band, The Grafton Showband from Cookstown – I don't think they ever played in the south but they would have been doing five nights a week in Ulster. It wasn't necessarily a political thing, it was just that they had plenty of work without coming down. Derry had literally dozens of bands.

Another region was the sunny south-east around Waterford and Wexford where of course you had The Royal who were the trendsetters and went on to achieve international success. But Waterford also provided us with The Blue Aces who were also very good and were known nationwide. This region also had bands like The Foot Tappers, Decca, Savoy, Fontana, The Derek Joys Band and another called The Atlantic who were resident in Tramore, featuring a young Dave Coady on trumpet and vocals, who would later feature with Donie Collins, The Real McCoy and The Big 8. From nearby Kilkenny came The Black Aces, The Nomads, The Jim Cantwell Band and later on The Tweed.

Around the midlands you had The Drifters as the big one from Mullingar, but you also had the smaller bands like Sid Shine in Athlone who played within their own little radius. Again, in the west you had The Premier Aces from Roscommon who were very big, playing five and six nights a week in the early 1960s. They would play the North on odd Saturdays because at that time there was no Saturday dancing in the south. But midweek, The Premiers would be packing them into all the small, local parochial halls along the west coast. Eventually, when their singer Micky Slymon emigrated to Australia, they got in this big name from England, someone who was a bit over the hill over there. Houston Wells was the guy's name, he had chart success in the UK with a song called 'Only the Heartaches' and he gave The Premiers a complete new lease of life and launched them to a higher level nationally.

That's not to say that they wouldn't have played in Cork and the North, of course they would, but generally 70 per cent of their business would have been in the western region where they were as big as any of the big bands. Each of these individual regional bands, like The Premier Aces along the west and The Michael O'Callaghan Band in the south, could hold their own against any of the other national bands from the other regions.

So, while all the top 20 bands played in main venues all over the 32 counties, when they went into these regions they also had to deal with the local heroes. Whenever a new band started, like The Royal Blues in Claremorris, they'd become popular locally very quickly but then it could take a little longer before they would take off in other areas. Big Tom was another example; they were based near Castleblayney in Monaghan and started to build up a local following and the word got out. And when the word got out, you were laughing, provided of course that it was the good word.

That's how it was. Every region would have this favourite local band which was great really. But it also confused things to a degree. You could be in the top five in your own spot and not be in the top 35 elsewhere. Other good examples of regional bands were The Regal from Cork, The Mighty Rhythm Boys from Buncrana, The Maurice Lynch Band from Castleblayney, The Woodpeckers from Dundalk and The Black Aces from Kilkenny.

When a band decided to split, over musical policy of course, they often became two bands. The Sands were a breakaway from The Miami, The Swallows came from The Premier Aces and then, later on, The Swallows became The Magic Band.

This was as we were moving through the 1970s and were getting into the Eighties when a lot of the gimmicks were getting ridiculous, but I will talk about this later.

Various Styles

The city slickers would have been Capitol, Miami, Pacific, Caroline, Airchords, Nevada (formally Jets), Cadets, Casino, Chessmen, Graduates, Millionaires, Kings, Jim Farley's Band, Express, Carousel, Ravens, Royal Earls, and Altonaires.

The Freshmen were a great pop band, as were The Real McCoy, Plattermen, Times, Sands, Casino, Caroline, Nevada.

Rural Bands

Outside the major cities were the likes of The Johnny Flynn Band, Joe Dolan and The Drifters, and The Royal Blues. Now, The Mighty Avons would be considered a kind of country band. In other words their emphasis would be more on country and western because of their singer Larry Cunningham, whereas say The Miami would be pop. Dickie Rock was a pop and big ballad singer and that would be the kind of distinction there. The Mighty Avons would play some pop stuff just like The Miami might play a little bit of country stuff, but The Miami was a pop band, like The Real McCoy was a pop band. The Mighty Avons and The Mainliners, they were country bands.

For a while some of the orchestras survived alongside the showbands, mainly Mick Delahunty and Maurice Mulcahy, and others also like Johnny Quigley, Gay McIntyre, Dave Glover, Jim Cantwell, Earl Gill and Chris Lambe.

Then there was a group of consistently good musical bands like The Swingtime Aces from Athenry in Galway, Blue Aces from Waterford, Black Aces from Kilkenny, Rhythm Boys from Buncrana, with Tony Woods on vocals, Woodpeckers from Dundalk, Platters and Polka Dots from Omagh, Regal from Cork, Casino, Express and Caroline.

Northern Bands

In general, northern bands, in my humble opinion, were musically superior to their counterparts in the south. Ouch! I know that will start a row among my musical friends in the south, but I believe it to be true due mainly to the fact that they had the luxury of musical tuition in the schools. Also, because of the availability of AFN radio and the influence of the American Forces stationed in areas like Derry and Belfast. This would have given the local lads access to big band jazz and good country music. Another factor could have been the lack of employment especially around Derry. This gave the musicians plenty of time for forming bands and jamming. Phil Coulter wrote about this phenomenon in his song, 'The Town I Loved So Well'.

Mutual Admiration Society

We called them the northern bands, while they, in turn, referred to us as the Free State or southern bands. While we envied and admired their musical ability they, on the other hand, were fascinated with the commercial sound and success of the likes of The Royal and The Cadets.

Support Bands and Relief Groups

The old 'support band' thing was instrumental in introducing a load of acts that subsequently became very popular. For instance, I remember Big Tom playing support in Rockorry on the Cavan/Monaghan border, also Skid Row with Phil Lynott and Brush Shiels in the line-up playing support to The Millionaires in the Atlantic Ballroom in Tramore. When Johnny Flynn was touring England he had a young band called Herman's Hermits playing support at the Astoria in Manchester for £15, and also Van Morrison and Them played before him at the Lyceum in London.

Almost everyone has a story like that, 'I remember when he/she played support to us.'

So these things happened, big deal, it just makes nice story telling. I reckon most bands had a claim to fame that, before they were heard of, Joe Bloggs and so and so played support to them.

Beat Groups

With the emergence of the beat groups and ballad singers during the mid 1960s, a slight tension developed as the new kids on the block looked with envy at the commercial success of the showbands.

While the showbands had the ballrooms and the marquee circuit at their disposal, and with the ballad scene finding a natural home in the emerging cabaret and lounge bar circuit, the venues for beat groups were somewhat limited. Apart from the major cities like Dublin, Belfast, Derry, Cork, Limerick and Galway, the rest of the country barely offered a dozen or so beat club venues.

So, while they may not have liked the music that showbands played, they certainly liked the money they were paid and that's why so many of the groups eventually adjusted their formats or joined showbands to play the ballroom circuit.

Ballad Groups

When the folk and ballad groups began to take off, a whole new area of entertainment opened up in the singing lounge and folk club scene. While it didn't clash directly with the dances, as the ballad sessions were run during pub hours, it did however push the dancing hours back to the later starting time of 11pm.

The ballad boom introduced us to a host of new performers, among them Johnny McEvoy, The Fureys, The Dubliners, Paul Brady, Christy Moore, Planxty and The Wolfe Tones. While, at the same time, the general cabaret lounge provided a platform for the likes of Foster and Allen, Brendan Shine and a host of others including a variety of comedians like Brendan Grace and Shay Healy.

Learning the Tunes

Down through the years, people would often ask how we prepared our music or learned our tunes; they would just be interested in how we went about it. I suppose it can be funny in a way when you start to think about it. Way back before the days of CDs and downloading music from the internet, the only way we could source new material was to tape the radio shows. One of the most popular shows was on Sunday afternoons at 4pm on BBC.

Alan Freeman was a great man for the pop charts. 'Hi there, Pop Pickers,' he'd say as he played his signature tune, 'Swinging Cymbals', before taking us through the Top 20 and whatever was bubbling under. It was a great opportunity for the bands who could tape that show, especially when he played the new releases from stars such as Cliff Richard and Elvis Presley. All the obvious ones, including The Beatles, who, whenever they released a new single, were almost certain to get into the Top 10.

When a song debuted at 29, you had it on tape immediately. Then you learned it so that when it made the Top 10, you already had it in your playlist.

Also on BBC there was a programme on Wednesdays at midday which featured the MLO, the Midland Light Orchestra, who would do a live band version on the radio of the Top 20 tunes. This was very beneficial for the showbands because if you had Cliff Richard and the Shadows, they would mainly be guitars and strings but the MLO would be using brass or saxophones to play the strings parts. Which is what we had to do, but it was great to have another version of it on tape. Sometimes, they were very intricate arrangements which you couldn't really copy, but they would give you the basic ideas anyway.

There were one or two funny stories because the MLO would actually be reading the pieces while playing them live. Like all live performances, they would get some of the pieces wrong. I remember a few classic clangers where the trumpet would come in where it shouldn't have. 'The Little Band Of Gold' is a song that comes to mind.

Music and Tuning Techniques

When we first started playing we had very little knowledge of the rudiments of music or the basic ground rules required in organising a musical combo.

In reality, everyone just learned their own bits and let it rip, hoping that it would gel together in some sort of a reasonable fashion. For example, we were not aware of the concept of 'concert pitch'. We didn't know that middle 'C' on the piano was the musical 'equator' so to speak, that we should all tune to this note and take our guidance from that point or pitch.

As we didn't have a piano in our band, the guitar player would tune to the trumpet or clarinet. When he would ask me to play an 'E' naturally, I would play my 'E' on the trumpet and then he would tune the guitar 'E' string to that note. Unfortunately, neither of us realised that an 'E' on guitar should have been 'F sharp' on the trumpet. In other words, guitars should tune to piano 'concert', while most 'brass' (trumpet, trombone, tenor sax) should pitch it one tone up.

So, for about three years, we all played merrily along, one tone below concert pitch. It was only when a new guitar player joined, and later when I moved to another band in Manchester that had a piano player, that all this came to light while rehearsing 'All My Loving' by The Beatles.

We had already been playing this song in the previous band using a basic chord structure. When my new musical friends started playing all these lovely minor and augmented chords, my eyes and ears were opened up to a whole new musical world of sound and harmony.

Getting the Words or Chords

Bands were often referred to as 'live jukeboxes' or 'yellow pack' versions of the international rock stars, so the learning of songs and new material was a big part of the musician's life. The art of getting the words or chords of a new song was the source of many a laugh, or indeed a good argument, over what were the exact words being sung by the various pop stars. While we thought some of our interpretations were bad, they were nothing when compared with the hilarious written requests that were handed up to us in the dancehalls, usually written on the back of a cigarette packet.

I will always remember the Carrolls No 1 cigarette packet, this was a great favorite, and you would get things written like, 'Please play "do you wanna taxi".' Meaning, of course, 'Tijuana Taxi'.

Another example was 'Educated Follower Of Fashion' by The Kinks, instead of 'Dedicated Follower of Fashion'. Then we'd get 'She's A Muscular Boy'. She's a muscular boy? 'She's A Must To Avoid' by Herman's Hermits. A favourite by The Beatles was 'Pay the Black Writer', which should have been 'Paperback Writer'. But the hard of hearing were not limited to the audience. When we were learning the words of Roy Orbison's 'Pretty Woman' one of the lads was sure The Big O was calling for 'Murphy' and not

'Mercy'! The same fella was convinced there was a big demand for Murphys out in Texas. Another of my favourites was John Denver's 'Sewerage Mountains' or 'Blue Ridge Mountains' of course. There certainly were a few gems.

Imagine five or six people gathered around a small tape recorder and each one listening for their own particular part. You'd have the singer trying to get the words, the guitar player listening for the chords, the brass players listening to the fill-ins and riffs, and all of them trying to get the music into their heads. Each one would be trying to zone in on their particular area and of course, everyone's part was different and everyone's part was the most important part.

You would have the singer wanting to stop the tape so he could write down that last line or two he had in his head, and the guitar player would be saying, 'No, no, let it run another bit, I want to get the next two chords there, just let it run to the next two bars.' And of course, God help the poor brass player that would try and have a little run at the piece. If they dared to get involved they would get their heads bitten off them. 'Nobody will hear a thing if you are blowing them old yokes in everybody's ear,' type of thing.

Each guy would be trying to concentrate on his particular area. So then, as soon as the guitar player had the chords or the singer had the words, 'Okay, let's try it out,' assuming that everybody else had their pieces. 'I'm ready now, so why isn't everybody else ready?'

You might hear the brass section saying, 'Could we just play the intro once more? To try and get the brass intro like.'

'What? Ye have been listening to it there for ages, have ye not got it off yet, hurry up.'

And as sure as hell, you would play it once or twice, you would have picked the key, 'Is that the right key?'

'Yes, it's grand.'

Of course, the singer would be pretty cautious at first getting the melody and the words. But he would settle and get more confident, finding that it was too high or too low, 'Can we change the key?'

The brass would have to go changing the key then. 'Why didn't you tell us that? Why didn't you pick the right key at the start?'

'What do you mean? Sure it's only up a tone, or down a half-inch, or up a half-inch. Are you able to play that yoke at all or not?'

During the rehearsals, for the first two runs, the singer would be cautious, but then when they started to get confident they would begin belting it out.

At rehearsals, it would be nice and quiet so they would be singing softly without straining themselves and would be getting low notes easy enough. But on the night in the ballroom, in the heat and the noise, they wouldn't hear themselves, so they would want to take it up or down a tone. But the awkward thing was, having learned it in one key, it was always difficult to change. You had to erase what you already had in your mind and then re-learn it in a different key which was tricky.

Genuinely, it is more difficult on a brass instrument than on a guitar or bass because really, with those, you just move up or down a fret or two. It may be not that simple I know, but it's something like that.

Also, as it usually took the singer a couple of nights to become familiar with the words, they would have to use a song sheet. The big problem was how to hide or camouflage the song sheet. Should we leave them on the floor, put them on a chair, pin them on the back of a speaker or even on the back of a lad's jacket that had to stand beside the singer?

The problem with leaving them on the floor was the fear of the local wiseguy who would see them and would start messing with them. If they were left just under the microphone stand he would of course turn them upside down or take them away making a big 'haw-haw' of the situation.

Another major issue when learning new material or songs would be the tempo of the tune. It was important to keep in mind that showbands were essentially dance bands and we played music for people to dance to. First you had the quick step, the dancers could jive to that. Then came the old time waltz and slow waltzes, followed by the slow foxtrots, foxtrots and tangos and a few 'mix 'em, gather 'em' yokes. It was a must to get the tempo right for the dancers. With this in mind, when rehearsing, very often one of the band would get down on the dance floor and do a role-play to check if the tempo of the new song was good for dancing to or not. I can remember on a few occasions when we would actually change the original tempo of a tune to make it more 'dancer friendly'.

In general, there was nothing better than a good off-beat to get them dancing and the most popular ones were jiving and waltzing. A drummer colleague once narrowed it down to two crucial tempos and described them as 'buff-cha, buff-cha, buff-cha, buff-cha' for the quickstep beat, and 'buff-cha-cha, buff-cha-

cha, buff-cha-cha' for the old time waltz beat. In other words, if you had two tempos you were near enough there.

It could be very funny at times watching from the stage, where you see how some couples just loved to jive and they would do the jive technique to everything that wasn't a waltz. Then there were other couples who would waltz to everything that wasn't a jive. Then you'd have the 'odd' couple who obviously didn't have a great sense of rhythm and instead of the regular 'one two three, one two three', for the waltz, they'd be going 'two three one', or even 'three two one, three two one'. But the most amazing feat of all was when one partner would be waltzing while the other did the foxtrot. While this was so comical and fascinating to watch, it never ceased to amaze me how, after starting on the wrong foot, they could persevere against the beat, right to the end of the song. It was like watching someone driving up a one-way street the wrong way, or going 'down' an 'up' escalator while trying to maintain a calm demeanor in the process; it was so funny to watch.

Occasionally, there might be a tune that would have a rather awkward introduction to it, or maybe a lead into the middle eight or bridge section, and some straight singers could have a problem with this. So, we would rearrange it by taking a longer run into that section, just to give the singer a better chance to make the change. Another ploy used in situations like this would be for one of the guys to stand behind the singer and count them through it, 'one two three, now'. If it was a fairly fast move they might miss it, so we would change it and this could make it better for the dancers also, but very often it was to give the singer a good run at it. Some bands would leave out a difficult section or a passage in a tune. Where there may have been a tune arranged for three trumpets, three saxophones and three trombones, here we'd be with a reduced line-up of one trumpet, one sax and one trombone and we trying to get the full sound of a Glenn Miller style band. Without the full voicing to cover the arrangements, it could be pretty tricky at times.

One tune that comes to mind was 'The Spanish Gypsy Dance' and there was one very well known band that decided to leave out its difficult part.

Another one by The Beatles was 'Strawberry Fields Forever'. That was a very popular song but it changed tempo a few times so it certainly wasn't very suitable as a dancing tempo and, as a result, very few bands attempted it. I remember one band in particular that did and it was said, 'God bless their innocence, do they know anything at all? Sure the people are not able to dance to that.'

That beautiful Peter Sarstead song 'Where Do You Go To My Lovely?' was also tricky. While it was in 3/4 time, it was neither an old time waltz nor a slow waltz. Some of the bands would play it as an old time waltz and you would just have to vary the tempo a bit. These were just a few examples.

I mentioned earlier about how some of the dancers would put funny names or titles on songs, but the bands themselves were not shy in making up titles or words, deliberately or otherwise. They would know the melody of a tune but might not know the lyrics. I remember one particular case where a guy (when there was a request for a song by Julio Iglesias) knew the melody of the tune but hadn't a clue about the lyrics. He sang the words of the 'Our Father' prayer in Irish to the melody of the tune. Talk about 'divine' inspiration, you just wouldn't know unless you were listening very carefully and most people didn't notice. Later, it developed into a bit of a party-piece for him.

Song List

At times you would wonder how some of the songs that were popular in the ballrooms came to be used in that particular scenario. I am thinking in particular of songs that Brendan Bowyer used in his repertoire, for instance, 'Love Thee Dearest', 'The Swallow', 'Boulavouge' and 'The Holy City'.

Bands played at that time for four to five hours at dances and sometimes a part-time band might only have a programme for two hours. It was also the era of the set of three tunes per dance, three quick steps, three slow foxtrots, three old time waltzes and so on. Everybody needed a few individual tunes on standby in the event of the band running low on the rehearsed tunes after a few hours. It was then a case of play anything you know.

So, the ever-ready shortlist could be a real mixed bag of musical allsorts. In Brendan Bowyer's case, as he was a trained singer who sang in a choir (his dad was a classical organist) and because he would have had access to a rather different style of music from dance or jazz music, I reckon it was a case of playing anything while something else was being organised in the background.

That would be an explanation for some of the songs that he pulled out of the bag like 'Boulavouge' which was in slow waltz tempo, and others like 'Love Thee Dearest', a slow foxtrot, and 'The Holy City'. Ironically, they became huge hits for him.

People just loved them but when you think of it, it was strange to have people going out for a night of dancing and light entertainment and here were these guys singing about 'Jerusalem' and the 'Croppy Boy'. Brendan once told me how these special items came to be included. He explained that 'Boulavogue' was a slow waltz. As regards 'Jerusalem', he said that when Jim Aiken first brought The Royal Showband to Belfast around 1960 for a Christmas party, they figured it would be something special for that night. It went down a storm and Brendan has been singing it ever since.

Then when other bands saw how well Brendan Bowyer was doing with this type of material, they decided to try it too. Some started looking for rebel songs, tragic songs and uplifting stuff such as 'Nobody's Child', 'Letter Edged In Black' and 'Rose of Roscommon is Blind'.

The list went from the sublime to the ridiculous as time moved on and it took things in another direction altogether. By the way, this is just an observation and is not intended in any way as a criticism of Brendan or his colleagues. It's just an example of how some bands' song lists became so varied because, believe me, I've been that soldier and have been in situations where we were on a five-hour gig and ran out of tunes after a while. Then it definitely was a case of, 'I know this tune, and let the rest of ye be thinking up a few more while we're playing. Then we'll start at the top of the list again.'

Five
Cutting Loose

Tours

The Paramount eventually negotiated their first tour of England. Our manager replied to an advertisement in the *Irish Independent*, we got the gig and off we went. This was around the summer of 1962 and, as very few of the bigger bands would tour during the high season at home with all the festivals and seaside resorts in full swing, the smaller bands had their chance. We were all aged between 15 and 20 and dying to get going.

We headed off from Tuam and I remember going to the North Wall in Dublin and there was none of these 'roll-on, roll-off' ferries at that time. The van had to be driven onto a contraption of a yoke, which would then be chained down and lifted by crane onto the cattle boat. I remember the driver had to stay in the van during this operation, which was a fairly daunting experience for him.

After we arrived in England, the first place we played was Birmingham. The promoter who organised the trip for us wasn't exactly a big-time operator and the first venue was actually a restaurant where they cleared out the tables and chairs to make way for the dancers. It was a nice enough location but it wasn't a regular dance venue. Anyway, it didn't matter to us, we were on a tour of England and to get playing anywhere was the main thing. A big deal for us was having a support band and this would be done by a group of Irish lads living in England. I remember some members of The Rooney Brothers band, a well established outfit on the Irish circuit, coming to see us that night. Their drummer, Mick Nash from Limerick, was a bit of a character who later went on to play with Roly Daniels and Jim Farley.

When the gig was over, Mick decided to bring a few of us back to our hotel and get something to eat on the way. We thought this was great as he had his own car, so off we set. He stopped off at what to me looked like a building site where this mobile chipper van was parked up.

'Right lads, I'll get ye something to eat now,' he says as he trotted over to this meals-on-wheels caravan. He came back with some takeaway stuff which, he informed us, was a steak and kidney pie. Well, mother of God, I never tasted anything so horrible in my life, I just couldn't eat it!

'You're not finishing that? OK, sure I'll eat it meself,' said the bould Mick, and he did.

Anyway, we christened it a 'steak and kill me pie' and from that day to this, I have never eaten a steak and kidney (or kill me) pie, no way José.

On that first night in Birmingham we wanted a memory of the opening gig of the tour so we invited the crowd to come up around the stage and we took photographs. I still have them and they tell stories in their own way.

The Bullring

There was a famous place in Birmingham called 'the Bullring'. It would be putting it mildly to say that it was a bigger version of Eyre Square in Galway. It had many lanes of traffic while we were just used to one lane at home. When we were trying to leave the city to get to the outskirts, we couldn't actually get off the Bullring as we kept running into the wrong lane and missing our exit. We kept going around and around. At the top of the Bullring was a bus stop and we passed that bus stop five times before we eventually got into the correct lane to take us out to Sparkhill or Small Heath or wherever we were trying to get to.

I remember the people at the bus stop noticed us, you couldn't miss the van with the name stuck on the side of it, 'The Paramount Showband from Galway'. They started to laugh when they saw us coming around the second time and third time, but after that we were hiding on the floor of the van because we were mortified.

St Bernard's

A tour might last for one or two weeks so that meant a bit of organising on the clothes and stagewear front as the three clean shirts would run out fairly fast. Pretty soon we had our first introduction to the magical workings of the launderette, but then again some lads would be too busy for that kind of thing. Every time I hear the Kris Kristofferson song 'Sunday Morning Coming Down' the memories come flooding back of some of our guys looking for their 'cleanest' dirty shirt.

Most of the time we wore white shirts and, as the tour progressed, there were various versions of 'white shirts' produced! Some of them were so bad that the lads would put on their jacket over the shirt, check which part of the shirt was showing and then get white chalk and rub it around the cuffs and collar to make it look whiter from the dance floor. While the shirt may have been manky dirty, from a distance, the chalk treatment made it look reasonably okay. What a breakthrough for science, hygiene and life on the road in general, with the invention of the magical drip-dry nylon shirt. God bless Marks and Sparks and St Bernard of Dunnes Stores.

One of the perks of travelling in the UK was the access to all night cafés, because this meant we could get something to eat on the way home from gigs.

We stayed in small hotels and B&Bs, some of which were okay but others were definitely suspect. I particularly remember one in Huddersfield where the beds were so damp that we had to sleep fully clothed, not to mention the greasy breakfast. One of our favourites was in Victoria in London which was always fairly busy because of its popularity with bands, truck drivers and bus drivers from the British Midland Bus Company. Sometimes when we arrived to check in we would be told, 'It's a bit early lads, the bus drivers are not up yet so you'll have to wait for another hour or two as we'll have to make up the beds.'

Talk about ships passing in the night, the bus drivers would be going one way and we'd be going the other, all hanging out in the same place.

Buffalo

Apart from the odd fiasco, these tours were generally good fun and we looked forward to them as they were like a holiday really. We got the opportunity of going to plush cinemas, shows, football matches or even shopping for new equipment. One of the first major venues I remember was in Camden Town, where Bill Fuller had a venue because the locality had a very strong Irish community and it was called the Buffalo. It actually had various names over a period of time as they kept changing for whatever reason. It was known as the Irish 32 Club, the Irish Town and Country Club, the Irish Centre and the Carousel Club.

My memory of one of our first visits was for a bank holiday weekend and the Saturday dance would be from 9pm to 5am. This was a two-band show where we would alternate with Tommy O'Brien's resident band every hour or two. Just imagine playing from 9 to 5 in the morning, but the Paddies would stay out all night. And why wouldn't they when they didn't have to go to work the next morning?

Like at home, there were no bars in the halls in those days. All that came later, so the dancers did their drinking in the local pub and came into the dance around 11pm. The Irish abroad loved to see the visiting bands and it always amazed me how attentive they were when the time came to play the anthem at the end of the night. English location or not, you played the Irish anthem only! Funnily enough, in the States we played both the Irish and the American anthems and the patrons were always thrilled to hear them and would often compliment us.

It was tough work but we loved it, and if we were asked would we do it all again? Of course we would; sure weren't we nearly famous!

The Fighting Irish

The English scene could be pretty rough at times. I am talking now mainly about the early 1960s when the Paddies living in England were heavy drinkers and known for fighting. Unfortunately, a lot of it was true as I have to say that down through the years, I did see a lot of fighting and rough scenes. When you are 15 or 16 years of age, it gives you an awful impression.

Some of the most violent fights that I have seen were in the Irish halls, to name a few there was the Banba in Kilburn and the Buffalo in Camden Town. I remember chairs being used in the Banba. In some places they would actually have an alarm bell on the stage. As soon as a fight would break out, we would have to press the bell which would ring out beside the bouncers on the front door. They would realise there was a furore going on and come in and sort it out.

But sometimes they were slow enough to come in and you would be ringing and ringing the bell. I remember going out to them at one stage and they said, 'Oh, we're coming in now.'

Somebody explained to me the theory behind the delay. They would let the punters fight away for a while and eventually, when they had themselves sort of 'boxed out of it', the big boys would come in and just do the macho bit, put them under their arms, hit them one swipe and throw them out. If the bouncers went in too soon, the lads might have their tails up and give them a bit of a hiding themselves. I suppose it was one of the tricks of the trade of being a bouncer.

But it wasn't unknown for what they called 'the Paddywagons' to be lined up outside the halls of Irish clubs at weekend nights.

When the fights started and the boys were thrown out, the police would pounce on them straight away and take them to the clink. It is an awful reflection on the Irish society really, but it did happen.

I remember seeing it in one hall in particular, the 32 Club in Harlesden which was a pretty rough spot and it was another one of the late gigs. We often played two dances in the one night; first we would play at Leytenstone from 9pm to 11pm. This was quite near one of the big hospitals and obviously there were a lot of nurses staying locally who would be big dancers. So, you would play there, finish at 11pm and head on back to London to play maybe from 1am to 3am in the 32 Club.

There was always the drag of shifting the gear. You had to take it down in Leytenstone after you'd finished, load it into the van, drive back into Harlesden, carry it into the 32, where the dance was already underway with the resident band, heave it up through the crowds and onto the stage. At that time, we didn't have any roadies so it was tough going having to do all the humping of the gear ourselves.

The night that sticks in my mind in the 32 was when they had renovated the toilets with brand new wash-hand basins, plumbing, the lot. We went into the gents' loo at the start of the gig and marvelled at the lovely new toilets and sinks. After the gig, when we returned to the toilets to change, the place was completely ripped apart. It was just pathetic to think that they only lasted one night. It was as if the punters said, 'How dare they put in new sinks and new toilets?'

They pulled out the pipes, the sinks and the toilets and kicked in the doors; it was savage. At times like these you'd say to yourself, it's no wonder the British think we're a rough lot. You would wonder what the point of it all was.

Tricks of the Trade

At times, there were great rivalries between the different ballrooms and promoters in the Irish clubs. One time, while we were the resident band in Manchester during one Lent, a promoter in Coventry had booked Locarno, which was the local Mecca ballroom. He had hired it to run a dance, an Irish night. He had Donie Collins down to play and had advertised as such, but there was some mix-up along the way and Donie couldn't appear. The promoter still had to put on a band so he contacted the ballroom in Manchester who arranged for the resident band, ourselves, to travel down and play as a 'visiting' band in Coventry. The promoter actually came up from Coventry to collect us because we were a resident band and had no transport. He also arranged for us to use the house PA in the ballroom and told us to think of a name on our way down.

I thought a good one to go with would be the name of some petrol brand and we all watched out for some inspirational signs as we travelled along. Anyway, we discussed our future band name in great detail along the way before settling on The Regency Showband, direct from Galway. So, if you were lucky enough to be in the Locarno Ballroom in Coventry, on St Patrick's night 1964, then you had the pleasure of dancing to yours truly, with The Regency, for one night only.

When we got there the promoter had a big sign up which read, 'Due to unforeseen circumstances of sickness, Donie Collins is unable to appear. However, we have a fantastic new band appearing instead . . .'

The venue had a resident band and we played as the 'visiting' Irish showband. It was a great night.

Locarno was part of the English Mecca chain of ballrooms which wasn't a regular Irish venue. The night we played there only added to an already nasty feud going on between two promoters. As arranged, our promoter guy was to drive us back to Manchester but when we went to drive away the van wouldn't start. He discovered that a bag of sugar had been put into the petrol tank and, from what I gather, that destroyed the engine. He arranged for a second van to take us home but imagine a bag of sugar being poured into the petrol tank! These were the little tricks of the trade in 'how to handle the opposition'.

The Sharrocks

On the first occasion I played in Manchester, around 1962, one of the most popular Irish venues was called The Sharrocks. It was owned and promoted by a man called Bill Connell in an old part of Manchester called Moss Side.

The venue was very old and the story goes that there was a gang of lads standing at the bar on the night of a dance when a bit of mortar fell down on one guy's shoulder. He started to complain about his good suit being ruined, so Bill took him aside, put a few quid in his pocket and promised him free admission for life if he didn't say anything to avoid the place being condemned.

Bill Connell and his brothers, who I think were Mayomen, were in the building business or, more specifically, the demolition business. They had a contract to demolish old parts of Manchester as there were lots of old housing estates that were zoned for demolition, 'pulling England down and building it up again' so to speak. Now, as it happened, The Sharrocks was located in the middle of the area in Moss Side which was zoned for clearing and, as Bill had the job of flattening the area, he intended to leave the dance hall until the very last.

Eventually, when it had to go, Bill bought another cinema up in Stockport Road which became the New Sharrocks, and eventually the Ard Rí Club. Again, he worked the old cinema trick, took out the seats and put in a maple floor and he had the perfect ballroom. Everything else was in place: the toilets, the stage, the seats and the cash box – the whole bit.

Some years later, I remember going back to play for the Connell brothers and as we approached the venue we found ourselves suddenly in the midst of a complete open space, the size of a couple of Croke Parks together. There were still roads to drive on, but no houses, just acres and acres of vacant ground. Smack in the middle of this wasteland stood one building: the Ard Rí Club.

Bill had knocked half of Moss Side and he left the ballroom there as long as he could, but eventually it too fell to the wrecking ball. It may not have been the biggest venue, but it had the biggest car park in the world.

The Long Weekend at the Buffalo Ballroom in Camden Town
Occasionally, we would be booked for a short tour such as a long Bank Holiday weekend which would take in the Friday, Saturday, Sunday and Monday.

Bill Fuller had two venues in England, the Astoria in Manchester and the Buffalo in Camden Town (or the Carousel, which it was later called as he kept changing the name).

Anyway, he would fly us over for the weekend on the Friday morning. Possibly, you would fly to London and do the Friday and Saturday there, and he would have a similar situation with another band flying into Manchester. Then the two bands would swap over for Sunday and Monday.

On one occasion, the arrangement was that on the Sunday afternoon, Bill Foley, who was the manager in London, would drive us to the top of the M1 motorway near Birmingham. He had arranged for the band in Manchester to travel south and meet us at an agreed point where we would swap over. Unfortunately, communications between the two organisers weren't the best because we were left waiting at a roundabout with no sign of the other band, who were obviously idling at some other roundabout. Time was running out and we had to be driven all the way to Manchester and hope that the other band had made it to London.

The idea was good in principle: two nights in London and two nights in Manchester. It was a great set up in London because Bill was bringing visiting bands over for weekends and it was a package tour, all-in flights and accommodation. The promoter actually provided the accommodation in a flat over the ballroom. There were two or three bedrooms and always a fridge full of food when you'd arrive. It was lovely, a clean place with all mod cons. By the time you were leaving, it would be in some state. It was right in the middle of Camden Town and I will always remember, there was a little cinema right across the road from us. I can vividly recall going to see Cliff Richard in *Summer Holiday* there.

I was fascinated with the cinema being right across the road from me. I also remember going on my own when the lads would be gone off for a drink or whatever; they wouldn't be that keen on going to the pictures. Maybe you would get one or two to go with you the odd time but I remember on that occasion, I was at the cinema on my own, with less than a dozen punters in the whole place on a lovely sunny afternoon.

The Curse of Emigration

Emigration was very much a way of life in the1960s, especially from the rural areas in the west of Ireland from Donegal right down through Sligo, Mayo, Galway, Clare and Kerry. It affected the whole country but particularly the west coast and there was a big demand for the bands to tour overseas to keep emigrants in touch with home. While they would have their resident bands in the ballrooms, it was a welcome change when a touring Irish band came to play at the major cities. But even the smaller towns like Bristol, Swindon and Gloucester had Irish clubs or centres.

The bigger cities had ballrooms, like the Banba in Coventry; the Astoria/Carousel in Manchester, the Harp and Shamrock in Birmingham, which was a two-tier set up, with a ballroom on each floor. There was a céilí band on one floor and the modern showband on the other. I will always remember the céilí band there because they had a black singer. He used to sing 'The Old Bog Road' and, in the 'modern' ballroom, where they had a resident band, they also had a black singer called Earl Jordan. He later came to Ireland to play with The Derek Joys Showband and also The Caroline for a while.

Well, there were Irish clubs everywhere. The Shamrock, the Blarney, the Emerald, the Banba and the Glacamara. I remember the Shamrock in Ealing, the Elephant and Castle, the Galtymore, the Emerald in Hammersmith, where there was also the Garryowen right next to the Hammersmith Palais!

This was a Mecca Ballroom where Joe Loss used to play and The Royal Showband had a big night there one Paddy's Night. But everywhere had an Irish centre. Manchester had the Sharrocks, the Astoria and also St Brendan's Irish Club and later the Ard Rí Club on Stockport Road.

Never Ending Tours of Survival

Touring was great for the bands and if a tour could be arranged, especially during Lent, it was a great source of revenue for survival because back then, as I've said before, there was no dancing during the seven weeks of Lent. It was a good thing to get away from the regular circuit for a week or two, it was like a bit of a holiday and it also filled in the quieter times. The quiet season would start around the end of September so you could say that October to Easter was the off-season at home, except for a few weeks around Christmas.

You would always try and arrange a tour in October and another one in March, to tie in around Paddy's weekend. The October one would tide you over to Christmas. You would have a busy time around Christmas and then things would slacken off again in January, February and March.

There were different levels of course. Some of the bigger bands would just go for weekends, maybe four or five days, but the lower division bands might travel for two or three weeks at a time. They would take in Scotland and Wales and some of them might even go to the Orkney Islands off Scotland. Very often, you would finish your tour in England on a Sunday night and then travel to Holyhead or maybe Liverpool on Monday to make the ferry for Dublin.

I remember on one occasion, in the mid 1970s, we had the Volkswagen with the trailer at the back for the gear and we were booting it back from London right up the M1 onto the M6 into Liverpool. But I remember we got two punctures on the trailer, two of the tyres weren't great. We just scraped in with about 15 minutes to spare. We met Paddy Cole and the lads and they were on deck watching us coming in and they said, 'Jaysus lads, ye were lucky, ye just barely made it.'

As things turned out, were we sorry we did. If I had known what was ahead of us, I would have punctured a few more tyres and missed it by 20 minutes; we wound up spending 22 hours or so on the ferry.

There was a ferocious storm. We had berths and I remember going to bed at about 11pm and waking up around 5am thinking, 'We're in, this is great, and I never felt a thing.' I looked out the porthole and we were right beside the dock so I began to get up.

Mulhaire said to me, 'Get back into bed, we haven't moved at all yet.'

We were still in Liverpool. It was an awful crossing. I could handle most things but I remember during that trip being tossed all over the place. I just had to lie down and we were to play that night in the Irish Club for Con O'Mahony. We had to ring him and say we weren't going to make it.

We went up to the captain's deck where they had this radio-phone and we got Con on the phone. As it was a radio, you would say something and then 'over' and it was desperate trying to get the message across.

That night, an eternally youthful female vocalist was attempting the crossing with us and she was trying to ring her beloved boyfriend. She had a date on the Monday so she had to ring her darling and cancel out because we were being thrown all over the Irish Sea. The cruel sea doesn't recognise stardom!

Mothercare

In latter years, the tour might be a ten-day event but what came into vogue in the Irish pubs was entertainment such as four-piece bands and the like. The Sunday morning gig became a good feature for middle-of-the-road bands. The idea was that, as you were over there, you might as well be working. So, you would play on the Sunday morning but very often you might have to come back from Birmingham on the Saturday night to play a lunchtime session in a pub in London from noon to 2pm.

The danger was that the lads would have a few scoops on empty stomachs, as generally we'd just get up and head straight down to the gig without even a cup of coffee. Of course, some of the lads found new buddies who would arrive to take care of them by taking them on to other clubs or maybe even to the cinema where everyone could fall asleep.

So, we could go to the pictures or back to the pad and into bed because we would be tired after coming back from Birmingham with only four or five hours sleep. Also, you might be playing that night, often in the Gresham and the following day you would have that long trip to Liverpool to catch the ferry home.

Of course, the Monday morning shopping spree had to be done with the usual mad panic for the Mothercare shopping list. The big fear always was what kind of a state would the lads be in when they'd arrive at the Gresham that night after a leisurely afternoon on the town with their buddies. This was the place with the revolving bandstand and, invariably, there would be one or two who would have gone a little over the top and they would be in mighty spirits. So much so, that when they would come to the revolving bandstand, somebody might be missing or a speaker could be left behind. The last gig in the Gresham was always a major headache, for me anyway. Everybody else was having a great time, well, maybe not everybody else, but there was always one night, generally the last night, when there would be major headaches.

From Shopping Malls to Transport Cafés

There is many a fine story from the shopping malls.

'We're going down shopping now to get a few presents,' would be the cry. There would be a group which, after a while, would have to split into twos because everyone would want to go in different directions, driving each other cracked. But there were some funny stories. On the motorways, there were those transport cafés. It was like 'move along and serve yourself' kind of thing. You had a tray and you would gather your bits as you crept along and, eventually, you arrived at the cash desk and paid for everything you had. It wasn't unknown for some of the lads to be sampling the wares on the way. A sausage roll and maybe even a glass of milk and as you would get close to the cashier, an empty glass or plate could be seen left back in amongst the sausages or cornflakes. So, with half the meal eaten, 'a coffee and a doughnut' would be declared to the cashier.

Sometimes at the entrance to these motorway cafés where some of the football coaches would frequent, you would see notices reading, 'No Manchester City buses, thank you' or 'No Arsenal buses, thank you'.

I'd say it wouldn't be long before there would be a few signs demanding, 'No showband buses, thank you'!

Howya?

From a business point of view, I built up a file of contacts for each venue including the names of the manager or bar manager or whoever else it was useful to remember. This might be considered cynical but it was initially to make things easier when you were ringing up to book as we were booking direct, so it was handy to have contact names. It was just like in any business; as a sales representative you would have the secretary's name, the manager's name and who the booking agent was. However, we would expand the file a bit to include the names of people who worked in the bar and the caretaker. Travelling to Bristol or Coventry or wherever, somebody would say, 'Oh, I was very friendly with what-was-his-name behind the bar?'

And the 'little black book' would be out, 'The doorman is Peter, the barmen are John and Kevin, so-and-so's wife's name is Eileen and the drummer with the resident band is Mick.'

It may seem a bit calculating but it wasn't. I mean you would have built up a friendship with these people but when you were playing in up to 20 different venues, it was impossible to remember everybody's name. We would have the little 'crash course' going along in the van when moving from one venue to the next so when we arrived we could say, 'Howya Mick?' or 'How's things, John? I see ye painted the place.'

'Jaysus, how well ye remembered my name!'

That was it, the politics of showbiz.

Stopping for Sweets

When going to Scotland, we would travel Larne to Stranraer. If you were playing Wales, you might go from Rosslare into Swansea.

There's a story told about a band that had two modes of transport, one van for the equipment and then the personnel carrier, a minibus the guys travelled in. Two guys would go in the equipment van and they might head off before the other one. One time, when the personnel guys arrived in Rosslare and got on board the ferry, they noticed that the other lads, the ones who had set out before them, hadn't actually arrived yet with the gear. They were watching and waiting as time was getting tight, but still no sign of the boys in the second minibus. Sure enough, departure time arrived and all the vehicles were on so the boat locked up and pulled off. The lads were hoping that maybe the equipment van was on board and the other lads were out of sight somewhere. Anyway, they had just pulled away from the dock when tearing down the road comes the van with the equipment, and the two boys in an awful state. The lads were up on deck looking down on the other two with the equipment van, they couldn't even shout at them as the ferry had moved away.

So, the boys in the equipment van had to drive from Rosslare right up to Larne, about 15 miles north of Belfast. They crossed over to Stranraer and drove from there right down through the north of England to Preston, took a right into north Wales to Newport and then tore up to the venue. They literally made it with, I think, about half an hour to spare. The band was in the band room sweating blood when the two boys arrived with the gear.

When they were asked what happened and what delayed them, one of the boys answered, 'We stopped for sweets.'

They obviously got lost but the driver would not admit it because he was supposed to know every byroad in Ireland. 'We stopped for sweets.' Can you just imagine the reception that got?

'Was it Smarties ye got or Emerald Greens?'

'Have ye any left?'

On the Boat

Generally speaking, we travelled from the North Wall to Liverpool and it wasn't that bad. It was a nine or ten hour trip, so we would book berths and go to bed at 11pm, get up at 6am, have something to eat, get the van off the boat and feel the tour had started.

You were off the boat between 7am and 8am, depending on how busy it was with trucks and where you were positioned in the ferry. Of course, the lads would have a few drinks as it was usually on the night off we would travel, and they'd be playing cards while having the few scoops.

We would allocate the tickets and the berths were colour coded. There was blue 234 or yellow 698 and so on and you would have two or three guys in each berth.

First thing, before they would get too tight, everyone would be given their tickets. If you didn't do this there would be all sorts of confusion later. We might have two berths with four in each. The non-drinkers would go to bed early and they would be telling the other lads, 'Don't forget now, its blue 234 you are in, right?'

Sure enough, some time around 3am, there would be banging at the door, 'Let me in.'

'You're not in this one.'

'Where did you say we were again? Is it yellow 248?'

This happened two or three times and apparently the guys would never actually go to bed. They would sleep on a couch somewhere.

So, we were paying for berths and they weren't using them but still they were waking you up trying to find out which berth they were supposed to be in. Then, one day the lads were doing the old economics and they realised, 'It is a waste of money getting berths for us seeing that we do not use them. What we will do is, don't bother getting berths for us, just give us the money instead.'

This was agreed and it was tried out a few times. But, when you were going onto the boat, you would be checked and the officers would see how many boarding tickets you had. If you had only four boarding tickets and there were six guys in the van, they would want to know why. So, we would get the four tickets and the deal was that two of the boys would hide to avoid being counted. They would lie down in the back of the van and we would put the suit covers over them.

When you would check in with the first guy, it was grand.

Then there was a bit of a drive before you came to the next checkpoint just before you got onto the boat, maybe it was half a mile, but the lads would be down on the floor hiding.

'Can we get up?'

'No, no, hold on a second, we have to come to another security guy.'

We would keep them down as long as possible, they wouldn't have to be down half that length of time but we would just keep them down for the craic.

'Hurry up, we're smothering. Can we get up now?'

'No, no, we're coming up to the guy now.'

And this would go on and on. The poor lads would almost suffocate all just to get the extra few quid for the jars. We had many good laughs out of that one and it gave a total different slant to 'travelling economy class'.

When we arrived in Liverpool, those who were organised would get up at 6.30am, go down to the canteen and have the breakfast. Then go to the van and wait in the queue to disembark. But you would be waiting for the stragglers to arrive down at the van. Some of them would arrive late for breakfast, others wouldn't even go for breakfast, but eventually it got to the stage when we would have to drive off. There were four lanes of traffic leaving the ferry and they would take one lane at a time. When your lane was moving, you had to move off and we would wait on the docks for the lads.

I remember on one or two occasions, a few of the boys would be late getting up and they wouldn't be the best after the night before and there was hassle with them getting off the boat. There were detectives there because this was the 1970s and there was a lot of trouble going on. The police would be checking identities because they were on the lookout for IRA guys. This caused hassle because more than likely the lads' identification papers were in the van, so sometimes there would be a bit of pressure.

Somebody had a bright idea; they would bring a photograph of the band in their pockets. I remember sitting in the van watching as they tried to get through security with the detective saying, 'Hold it there.'

And the boys would produce this photograph and say, 'That's me there in the photograph.'

The detectives would look at the state of them. They no more looked like they did in the photograph where they were all groomed and dolled up and now they were like something the cat dragged in on a wet night.

But somehow they always succeeded in getting through!

Six
Over the Waves

When I was 17

During January 1964, The Paramount went on a short tour of England mainly around the Manchester, Birmingham area. By this time, the band was into its fourth year and things were beginning to slide a bit. Some of the original members had moved on to other bands and, as it happens, we were finding it harder to get regular work which meant having to travel further afield on a regular basis. Not that this was a major problem as most bands loved the tours but it did mean that you couldn't always get a gig in the preferred or main venue in the region. Two reasons for this were that bigger acts might be booked in, or the promoter might not want you overplaying an area because the novelty or demand for your particular band would wear thin. This, of course, made good business sense.

One thing to remember as regards the Irish in England and

the US, just as with the GAA, was that tribalism was a big thing. By that, I mean it did have an impact on the dancers and punters as to where the visiting band was from. For example, most emigrants were from the western counties: Galway, Mayo, Leitrim, Donegal, Clare or Kerry. So, the promoter had to balance his diary – if he had a Galway band one weekend, then he would try to book a Mayo band for the next week and a Donegal or northern band after that and so on, within reason.

Another angle on it would be the fact that people from certain counties tended to settle in certain areas. You would find a lot of Mayo and Galway people around Manchester and Leeds while the Dublin people seemed to head for Liverpool and Birmingham.

In Boston you'd find a lot of Galway and Kerry people, while Cleveland Ohio was a huge Mayo stronghold. As for Scotland, sure it's full of Donegal people.

Getting back to the UK trip in January 1964, as we couldn't secure a booking in the leading Irish venue in Manchester, the Astoria, (Bill Fuller's place) we were booked into the next big venue, the New Ard Rí on the Stockport Road.

As there was usually a support band on from 9pm to 11pm with the visiting band playing from 11pm to 1am, I had time to call and visit my friends at the Astoria in Plymouth Grove. The purpose of the visit was two-fold: to keep in touch with a view to future bookings, but also to see the musos in the resident band, especially my drumming buddy Chris Mullahy, who had left The Paramount to take the resident gig at the Astoria a few months earlier.

I had become pretty friendly with the Astoria staff during our visits there so they gave me a big welcome and made a bit of a fuss, which was nice. However, it was politely mentioned, now that we were playing in that 'other place' they wouldn't be able to book The Paramount in future to play in the Astoria.

After a very pleasant visit, I duly said my goodbyes and headed for the Stockport Road. It turned out to be quite a good gig and the gang from the Astoria called over to see us play after they handed over to their visiting band at 11pm. Afterwards, we all headed down to the local Chinese for a feed. Oh, the joys of being on tour in the big cities.

The next day we travelled to Coventry to play at the Banba, another converted cinema. I remember us playing 'Desafinado' a great jazz tune, much to the annoyance of our guitarist and vocalist, Colm Connolly, as we hadn't it properly rehearsed.

It was simply a case of our tenor sax player, Jimmy Reilly, who, having learned the tune for his own enjoyment, now found himself being asked to play it whenever we thought it might impress. Here we are in the Banba on a Sunday night in January 1964, sure weren't we bound to make a big impression on all the 'jazz heads' in the ballroom and they waltzing the night away. So what if our sax player Jimmy is the only one of us who knows the tune properly.

Anyway, during the night I was called to the phone, phew! Panic! It was the gang from the Astoria in Manchester offering me a job. Would I like to be bandleader of their resident band?

Would a cat drink milk, is the Pope a catholic? And all that Jazz! Put that in your pipe and smoke it, food for thought when I was 17.

The International

A decision was reached to disband The Paramount and I played drums for our final gig in the Crystal Ballroom in Kiltormer on Shrove Tuesday in February 1964. I got back from the gig at around 3.30am, packed my gear and headed off for Manchester to become leader of the resident band at the Astoria.

As a 17 year old I was chuffed to find myself playing support to all the top bands visiting from Ireland: The Capitol, Cadets, The Donie Collins Band, Polka Dots, Dixies, Swingtimes, Blue Aces, Royal Blues, Joe Dolan and the Drifters.

I distinctly remember the first night, as the visiting band was The Capitol, my big favourites and as bandleader, one of my duties was to act as MC. I found myself introducing my idols on stage on the very first occasion that I ever spoke into a microphone in public. As I mentioned, this was my debut with the resident band and it was arranged that on my formal introduction I would feature on a trumpet solo, so you can imagine how nerve wrecking this was for me knowing that The Capitol boys were about and they having within their ranks the wonderful trumpeter, Bram McCarthy.

I did, however, have the neck to check with Paddy Cole and Des Kelly to see if Bram would be doing any special feature. Des graciously asked me to pick my choice and they would avoid an overlap. It was typical of The Capitol gentlemen, professional and generous, so I reluctantly played a very nervous and timid version of 'The Lonely Bull' with my knees knocking at a frantic pace.

Over the next few weeks we put some serious work into rehearsing the band and, with the addition of some experienced players, we turned out to be quite entertaining. The word got out about this new outfit in Manchester and we started to receive offers to play at other Irish centres, so after due consideration we decided to quit our resident gig at the Astoria and launched ourselves as The International Showband on the Easter weekend of 1964.

Most of the work was in Irish halls in Manchester, Birmingham, Coventry, Liverpool, Leeds and London.

Initially, we based ourselves in Manchester but as time went by we found ourselves spending a good deal of our time in London. We took a flat there after a few months and alternated with Manchester for a while, before eventually settling in London.

The Irish circuit was pretty much the same as home as regards the programme of music. We would play whatever was in the Top 20 with a little Irish flavour thrown in. One big exception however, was the fact that most venues had a resident support band which meant you only had to play for two to three hours maximum, instead of the usual four or five hours at home. Generally speaking, the Irish halls are the same the world over.

As with all capital cities like Dublin and Belfast, London was the most hip and modern in the UK but outside of that you could close your eyes and you'd hardly know the difference. Most halls and ballrooms operated on Fridays, Saturdays and Sundays with the bigger city ones running Tuesday, Thursday and Sunday afternoons providing the lonely Irish with somewhere to go to get out of the digs or flat.

Each venue had a decent resident band, usually an eight- or ten-piece orchestra, and all readers. Palais bands, as they were known, in the style of The Joe Loss Orchestra at the

Hammersmith Palais, would cover the full gig except when there would be a visiting band from Ireland. The resident musicians were generally all accomplished English players with an odd Irish guy, usually a singer or MC, thrown in to keep manners on them.

You can imagine the big publicity poster outside the Irish Club: 'Dancing This Weekend, Friday, Saturday and Sunday, to the Resident Band plus Blarney Céilí Band. Friday night special, direct from County Galway, the fantastic International Showband. Come and hear their great new record, "The Sheep's Farewell to the Mountain", now in the Irish Top 20.'

Our attempt to crack the English club scene was pretty feeble really. Our line-up included Irish, English, French, and American nationalities, plus we had two vocalists with the lead singer ten years older than me. There was no way I could control these guys.

However, I have to say that generally we all got on well and we definitely had some great times together. We did very well on the Irish scene but, as this was very limited, we soon began to suffer from the big fish in the small pool syndrome, so we knew we had to try to break new ground.

The beat scene was huge at the time, around 1964, and as rhythm and blues groups were four- or five-piece outfits, when we would arrive at a venue, an eight-piece band, we probably had the wrong image for the younger set. We were more geared for the cabaret or the working man's club scene.

Seven
Off to Germany

When bands talked about 'the tour', invariably they meant a tour of the North (the six counties) or England which would take in a bit of Wales or Scotland. Only the elite were brought out to America, the big names.

In 1964, I was living in England and playing with The International Showband. At that time a new market had opened up for the British groups to tour in Germany, playing in clubs and also some of the American bases. Occasionally, we would come across promoters who were booking bands and groups for the German market so, as luck would have it, we were offered a contract and were booked for a six-week tour of Germany. There was a 'Star Club' network if you like, and we were to start in the Star Club in Hamburg which was a famous venue. Lots of British groups played there, most notably The Beatles in their very early days. Because of that we thought, 'If we get to play in the Star

Club in Hamburg we're going to make it too, just like The Beatles!'

And so say all of us! Thousands of groups must have played there down through the years, and not too many of them went on to become international superstars.

So, as the Star Club become a big commercial name in the music business, they franchised out the 'brand name' to other regions and eventually they had other Star Clubs in places like Cologne, Kiel and Berlin. It was something like the Las Vegas Ballroom in Tuam and the Las Vegas Ballroom in Templemore and the Las Vegas Ballroom wherever.

Our six-week tour included a week in the Star Club in Hamburg, before going on to Kiel and Berlin and Cologne. We played the last weekend again in Hamburg before we returned home.

Visas

But a lot happened before we even got to Germany! The date was arranged and we set off from Manchester in a van with eight of us on board, including the manager.

Now, visas might have been a consideration, but we didn't have them organised at the time and were told it wouldn't be a problem if we had our passports. So, we headed down to Dover, sailed to Ostend in Belgium and then drove from there for two days with one stopover. We went from Belgium into Holland and I remember changing money a couple of times before eventually arriving at a German checkpoint. There were soldiers there and we had to wait our turn.

'Who are you and what are you doing?'

Throughout the Sixties, *Spotlight* magazine was the bible of the entertainment scene in Ireland. It was our version of *Melody Maker* and *NME*. It covered the Top 30 charts and with writers like Pascal Mooney, Shay Healy, Pat Egan and Julie Boyd, sure we couldn't go wrong!

Julie Boyd's page was a must for all the gossip. This page shows Jazz Coasters in the top middle photo, trumpeter Mick Nolan in the left-hand column and an advert for Big Tom in the centre.

The Smokey Mountain Ramblers featuring Pat Ely, George Kaye and Tommy Higgins.

Country music was always popular in Ireland and most bands included it in their repertoire, especially The Mighty Avons and The Mainliners. When Larry recorded Lovely Leitrim and Tom sang Gentle Mother on the showband show, the trend turned towards country and Irish. While the 1970's brought the Smokey's and Cotton Mill Boys playing Cajun country, the pop fans took another route and followed bands like The Plattermen, Chips, Real McCoy and The Memories.

When Larry Cunningham and the Mighty Avons recorded Eddie Masterson's 'Tribute to Jim Reeves', on the 'King' label, it was a huge success both at home and abroad. It actually reached the top 30 in the British charts! Larry recorded many hits including 'Lovely Leitrim', possibly his biggest hit of all.

Bands were always on the look-out for a photo opportunity. While in Boston in 1964, The International Showband got to visit the training camp of Cassius Clay/Muhammad Ali, who at the time was preparing for a world title fight with Sonny Liston. Our picture shows Betty and the boys getting the Champ's autograph. The guy second from right in the check shirt is Bill Warren of the 'New State Ballroom' where the band played.

The Millionaires meet Mayor Daly of Chicago in 1966. Daly was a very powerful man in American politics and it is said he played a major part in the election of President Kennedy. The mayor, whose son would later succeed him in City Hall, claimed to have Irish connections in Waterford. Our picture shows from left to right Michael O'Brien, Frank McGowan (tour promoter), Johnny Devitt (band manager), Mayor Daly, Gene Bannon, Joe Doherty, Jimmy Higgins, Mickey Conn and Billy Doyle.

The International Showband started out as the resident band at Manchester's Astoria/Carousal Club. As a result of many offers, they decided to go on the road and worked the many Irish clubs/centres throughout England. They toured Germany and the US, but they never actually got to play in Ireland. While they did have great success in the UK, the circuit was limited and they soon tired of the scene. When they disbanded, most of them returned to Ireland to join other bands. This picture shows (from left) Paul Chaurlton (Jim Farley), Frankie Dwyer (stayed in Manchester), Pat McDonald (Trixons/Donie Collins), Betty-Anne McCabe (Teenbeats), Chris Mullahy (Casino/Indians) Jimmy Higgins (Millionaires), P. Greene (Cadets), Eddie Howard (returned to America).

Some of The International 'stars' posing outside Bill Fuller's New State Ballroom in Boston. This famous venue was used for the ballroom scenes when filming the Glenn Miller Story. The support acts were The Diplomats and Des Regan's Céilí Band.

Maxi, Dick and Twink worked as a female vocal group on the cabaret circuit and as session singers on some of the big showband hits. The cabaret scene wasn't strong enough to contain the talented trio and as a result of many offers, the girls eventually moved into the ballroom scene with showbands. Maxi teamed up with Danny Doyle in Music Box. Dick sang with a revamped Royal after Brendan Bowyer and Tom Dunphy left to form the Big 8. Twink also joined the Big 8 in a star studded line-up that took them right to the top, both here in Ireland and in Las Vegas. Maxi now works in radio, Dick moved to Canada, while Twink is still a big name in the Irish entertainment industry.

Donegal band Margo and the Keynotes had a taste of chart success with their first record, 'Road by the River' and 'Bonny Irish Boy'. When Margo later signed to Ruby Records with The Country Folk she had many hit singles and albums. Her first number one was 'I'll forgive and I try to forget' and she was to become one of the biggest attractions on the country and Irish scene. It obviously ran in the family because her younger brother was later to become one of the biggest stars this country has ever produced, a certain gentleman called Daniel O'Donnell!

With pop and country taking different routes during the Seventies, the 'lads' were well represented on the country scene. However, with women's lib just around the corner, along came Philomena and a truckload of her female friends. Singers such as Susan McCann, Margo, Gloria, Sandie Kelly, Eileen King and many more, all aiming to be The 'Queen of Country Music'!

LP cover of Philomena Begley and The Country Flavour.

Based in Cork, The Victors were always a force to be reckoned with. Front man, Mr Personality himself, Art Supple, was a great entertainer. Backed by such musicians as Mickey Brennan on trombone and sax, Chris St. Leger and that great jazzman Len McCarthy, together they really produced some sound! The signing of Eurovision winner and ex-Skyrockets man Pat McGuigan was a major boost to The Victors. Pat's record company spelt his name 'McGeegan' to help the British disc jockeys with the pronunciation. When Pat's son, young Barry McGuigan started to box, they left him alone!

The Conquerors were one of Ireland's longest working bands and are still going strong despite some personnel changes along the way. What a lovely set of suits – definitely no chance of getting knocked down as you cross the road lads!

HOTLY TIPPED FOR THE TOP
The DONIE COLLINS Showband

featuring CHRIS
singing "Young Love"

B side "MEXICAN BOY"

ON SALE SHORT

A publicity poster for The Donie Collins Showband's new record 'Young Love/Mexican Boy' featuring Chris Grace on vocals. They reached Ireland's top ten. This Limerick-based outfit had another great singer in Austin Graham, who could sing anything from Jim Reeves to Roy Orbison with ease.

FIRST TIME NO.1

OLD MAN TROUBLE

DOC CARROLL and the ROYAL BLUES

SAY THANKS TO EVERYONE WHO HELPED MAKE OUR RECORD A SMASH HIT

U.S. TOUR VISITING FEB 24 · APRIL 2
NEW YORK · CHICAGO
BOSTON · SAN FRANCISCO

Another poster reminding The Royal Blues fans that following on the success of 'Old Man Trouble', Doc and the boys were off to the US on tour.

The Indians. Formally known as The Casino, these boys took the country by storm when they donned the war paint and feathers. A very entertaining band, with great singers and musicians, they were greeted with excitement everywhere they went. According to the latest smoke signals, they're still on the warpath.

From Belfast, The Mysterious Silhouettes. Keeping a low profile, these boys liked to keep us all in the dark!

When The Swallows flew back to Glenamaddy, Joe O'Neill waved his wand and 'hey presto' The Magic Band was born. With singer Kevin Walsh as 'Magic', the band were Mikey Belton, Joe Bernie, Frank Clancy, Mike Mannion, Vinnie Thomas and trumpeter Johnny Carroll.

Formally The Royal Earls, these boys went a bit wild for a while and were seen in many places acting as 'Zulus'. Eventually they calmed down and went back to playing music, I think!

Eddie Masterson
The legal eagle of the showband fraternity. He lived in Barry's Hotel in Dublin and held court there regularly. This is a photo of John Woodful's painting of the great man 'at the office'. Eddie liked to dabble in showbusiness and wrote the lyrics for the 'Tribute to Jim Reeves' recorded by Larry Cunningham and the Mighty Avons!

Frankie

Frankie 'Flash' Hannon (drummer/singer/ entertainer). Frankie played alongside Ollie Maloney in the great Johnny Flynn Band of the early Sixties. Famous for his great dancing 'off-beat' and impersonations of Fats Domino and Louis Armstrong, Frankie was always a highlight of the show. To put it another way, 'Frankie and Ollie were brilliant'.

Ollie Maloney – 'How'm I blowing Sham' this 'polaroid' pic was taken at a 'social' in Ryan's hotel in Tuam circa '63. At the back, Mickey Colohan of the famous guitar family can be seen.

Ollie and friends having a session at a fund-raising event for the Tuam Brass Band in the Imperial Hotel, Tuam, shortly before he passed away. Left: Michael Tuttle, Danny Kelly, Ollie, Tommy Ward, Jimmy Higgins, Tommy Dunne, Frank Donlon. This picture was taken by Liam Newman who was also a member of the original Tuam Brass Band.

Nevada with Red Hurley and Kelley

Formed in the mid Sixties the original Nevada (formerly The Jets) were led by sax man Tommy Hayden with his brother Peter on drums and Jim O'Connor on vocals/bass. When Tommy became the band's manager another brother, Bunty, took his place on sax. Consistent in being one of the country's top bands they always featured good strong vocalists. Names like Maisie McDaniel, Kelley, Tina, Roly Daniels, Red Hurley, Glen Curtin, Ronnie Medford and Rod Taylor all worked with the band at various times. Along with stalwarts like Peter and Jim, other long-serving members were guitarist Liam Hurley, Val Kearney on trombone and Willie Walshe on trumpet. As well as nurturing good musicians, some of the biggest names in Irish showbiz passed through the offices of Tommy Hayden Enterprise (T.H.E.), people such as Johnny Logan, Linda Martin and a young Mayo man, Louis Walsh.

Nevada with Tina and Glen Curtin.

Chessmen . . . spot Bobby Ballagh, the famous artist on the left, before he became really famous for selling his bass guitar to Phil Lynott!

Doc Carroll and the Nightrunners. Doc (third from left) with Tom Allen aka T.R. Dallas (second from left) without the cowboy hat and Tony Allen (extreme right), without Mick Foster!

Jim Tobin and the Firehouse
'Well, this is it', Big Jim sang sweetly on the Honey record label. He must have been right, will ya look at the lovely car they have. That's Donie Cassidy sitting on the bonnet. 'Hey lads, get offa my car!'

The Paramount from Tuam, where journalist Colm Connolly (front right) spent a while 'rocking 'n' rolling' before joining RTÉ.

Paddy Hanrahan and the Oklahoma from Longford featuring famous author, Pat McCabe (on left), before he got a proper job!

It's a stick-up !
That's why they're Millionaires

Our mock-up special is another young generation band feature

IT'S a hold-up! But the Millionaires don't really have to raid a bank to make a stack. They are one of the most promising of the young Irish showbands climbing, gradually but surely, to stardom.

The young Millionaires (average age 20) are lively, full of enthusiasm, and determined to please. They've got real music with a tip and a flair that has made them big favourites among discerning young people in Dublin ballrooms like the Crystal, Town and Country, Ierne . . . many parts of the country.

Every one of them—Gene Bannon (leader, sax, clarinet and pianette), Joe Doherty (bass guitar), Micky Coss (lead guitar), Michael O'Brien (drummer), Billy Doyle (trombone), Jimmy Higgins (trumpet) and Fergus Burke (lead vocalist)—can sing.

That's a lot of singers. But one of the biggest attractions of the outfit is the doubling of Joe Doherty and Micky Coss.

They were featured on the very successful disc "Winter Winds" (B side "Chime Bells"). And they plan more like this.

Manager Pat O'Flynn says of them: "They're young and bursting with enthusiasm. They put their whole hearts and souls into everything they do. They really live for music. That's one of the main reasons for their success.

"There have been together for less than three years, but in that time they have built up a huge following . . . rather quickly. If you could put it that way for a band with such unbounded energy and gradualness."

He and road manager John Devoy have earned along what they believe is a great talent. Said John: "We did not want to rush things. In bands, we feel, is disaster for those who have not developed their talents. The Millionaires have blended into a versatile musical outfit that will rise and stay at the top."

And that's an unrequisite line for drummer O'Brien . . . He's a gifted, really, a trained mike, he and his brothers own a mine which they fix themselves.

Hands Up . . . it's a stick-up
This feature in *Spotlight* magazine shows The Millionaires pulling a 'mock' bank raid on Dublin's Suffolk Street circa 1967. Take note of the three hard men, Mickey, Jimmy and Joe leaving the bank with the 'loot' and the 'worried faces' of Billy and Gene, as Fergie tries to control the getaway transport, a Guinness horse and cart. Innocent times indeed!

Vocalist Terry Cash was replaced by Fergie Burke. Drummer Alfie Merrigan replaced Michael O'Brien when he left to pursue a professional career in aviation. That's Michael sitting in the cockpit as a trainee pilot.

FOR A JACKPOT OF ENTERTAINMENT
NEW BLARNEY & KEYMANS CLUBS
PRESENTS

KEYMANS CLUB
4711 W. MADISON ST.
FRIDAY
JAN. 14th

NEW BLARNEY
87th & WOOD ST.
SAT. & SUN.
JAN. 15th & 16th

THE MILLIONAIRES
SHOWBAND
"DUBLIN'S NEWEST SHOWBAND SENSATION"
STRIKE IT RICH IN CHICAGO WITH MUSICAL RICHES

We're in the money . . . Showbiz! A licence to print your own money?
Bill Fuller's marketing man in New York, Joe Ruane, came up with this great gimmick to promote The Millionaires American tour. They distributed these hand-outs at the various venues for weeks before we arrived. We got a great kick out of them and they continued to use the idea every time we toured. Vocalist Penny Trent (centre) left to join the Skyrockets.

The many faces of the Capitol Showband. This record features big ballads, jazz, country, tangos. It is a real showcase of the talented individuals in the band. It typifies the versatility of this top class professional showband.

From Ballymena, the Freshmen were the first of what we might call a superband. Fronted by Derek Dean and Billy Brown they had a very modern approach to their performance! They had wonderful harmonies and a funky brass section. They moved away from the traditional showband styles in stage dress and repertoire. Just listen to some of the original material on this 'Mono' recording and I'm sure you'll agree that the Freshmen were definitely . . . 'movin on'!

Another northern band that based themselves in Dublin, Chips were a highly successful pop band. Led by the talented Paul Lyttle, with the great Linda Martin on vocals, and managed by the 'Guru' himself, Mr Louis Walsh, sure what more can I say!

Following his successful appearance on the TV show Jamboree on Telefis Éireann, Dermot O'Brien and his Clubmen received many offers of work from all over the country. With his recordings of songs such as the Galway Shawl, the Old Claddagh Ring and Merry Ploughboy, his popularity was to continue for decades before he moved to America.

What an array of talent featured on this album released on the Pye/Marble Arch label – Joe Dolan, Dickie Rock, Eileen Reid, Brendan O'Brien, Gerry Cronin, Derek Dean, Sean Dunphy, Sean Fagan.

Indian Country
This is The Indians' first album. It was released about a year after they took to the road and features a lot of the material they played at their dance gigs. Numbers like Indian Burial Ground, Squaws Along the Yukon, Wig Wam Wiggle, Apache etc. Recorded at both Eamonn Andrews and Trend Studios in Dublin, it was arranged and produced by Noel Kelehan.

Tony and the Graduates had a big hit song called Kelly, and when they came to record their first album they stuck with the winning title of Kelly, hence the big letters in Kelly green. The band was based in Skerries, near Dublin as most of the boys were from that locality. Like most bands they played the length and breadth of the country, as well as the odd tour of the UK and the US along the way. After the band folded, Tony took up teaching as his new profession.

'Ireland's Best are on Release' and browsing though this list of country singers you'd have to agree. There's Larry Cunningham, Tom Dunphy, Brian Coll, Ray Lynam, Dermot Hegarty, Brendan Shine – to name just a few.

While fronting The Times, the Swarbrigg brothers, Tommy and Jimmy, were always keen to write and record their own original material. As a result, most people were pleased when RTÉ picked one of their songs, 'That's What Friends Are For' to represent Ireland in the Eurovision Song Contest in 1975. They were back again in 1977 to join forces with Alma Carroll and Nicola Kerr when they came a respectable third with another Swarbrigg original 'It's Nice To Be In Love Again'.

The town of Tuam seemed to get a kick out of having two of everything. Two cathedrals, two archbishops, two boys' schools, CBS and St. Jarlath's, two girls' schools, Mercy and the Pres. Not to mention the two football greats, the terrible twins, Purcell and Stockwell! When we look at this page from the *Tuam Herald* dated August 10, 1963, we see two cinemas, the Mall and the Odeon, two dancehalls, the Phoenix and the Las Vegas. See also the two carnival adverts for Dunmore and Moycullen Festivals. For me, the striking thing about this page is the variety of entertainment at that time. With the Capitol and Blue Aces in Tooreen, Maisie McDaniel in Ballyhaunis, the Miami and the Kilfenora in the Las Vegas. For more céilí dancing we had Liam Ivory in Barnaderg, and also céilís in the Phoenix and Cummer. For the best in entertainment you had the Green Cinema in Dunmore while the Sawdoctors' hero Tommy Kaye ran his Teen Beat club on Friday 9th. Could this be Ireland's first disco show? Then to add to all this merriment you had C.I.E. inviting us all to Galway from Westport, on Sunday 18th for a return fee of 15/9. Such excitement!

WIN EVERY RECORD IN IRELAND'S TOP 30

A fabulous new contest in which you can use your skill and knowledge of the pop (and ballad) world to win a fantastic prize. It will be a weekly competition in which readers are asked to forecast the position in the following week's chart of a selected record. Generally it'll be one with potential that's just been issued or a disc that has just made it into the Top 30.

This week it's Tom Jones's "I'll Never Fall in Love Again". Where do you think it will be next week? That's where your knowledge and skill comes in ! You're the expert.

The contest is free. All you have to do is fill in the Number at which you think this disc will be next week. The prize: ALL THE RECORDS IN NEXT WEEK'S TOP 30.

They go to the reader with the first correct forecast out of the post. Entries must be in by Tuesday, August 15.

"I'll Never Fall in Love Again " will be No. ...... in next week's Top 30 Chart.

NAME ....

ADDRESS ....

....

Entries to Disc Forecast, New Spotlight, 85 Grafton Street, Dublin 2.

WINNER OF EVERY RECORD IN IRELAND'S TOP THIRTY. Vol. I. No. 11
The correct forecast for "All For Me Grog" was No 11. First correct entry opened was sent in by: MISS ETHEL BURNETT, Ballybug, Ballynacargy. Mullingar, Co. Westmeath.

this weeks TOP POPS
COMPILED & CERTIFIED BY CHARTERED ACCOUNTANTS

Played on Radio Caroline (257 metres) Saturdays 8.30 p.m.—10 p.m.

THIS WEEK	LAST WEEK			NO. OF WEEKS IN
1	(1)	ALL YOU NEED IS LOVE—The Beatles	Parlophone	4
2	(1)	BLACK VELVET BAND—Johnny Kelly, Capitol	Pye	11
3	(5)	TAR AND CEMENT—Joe Dolan and the Drifters	Pye	3
4	(6)	SAN FRANCISCO—Scott McKenzie	C.B.S.	3
5	(3)	SHE'D RATHER BE WITH ME—Turtles	London	7
6	(4)	ALTERNATE TITLE—The Monkees	R.C.A.	6
7	(7)	THERE GOES MY EVERYTHING —Englebert Humperdinck	Decca	9
8	(10)	BOSTON BURGLAR—Johnny McEvoy	Pye	14
9	(9)	LAND OF GINGER BREAD—Gregory and the Cadets	Pye	5
10	(15)	SEE EMILY PLAY—Pink Floyd	Columbia	4
11	(11)	ALL FOR ME GROG—Dubliners	Major Minor	6
12	(8)	A WHITER SHADE OF PALE—Procol Harum	Deram	10
13	(19)	IT MUST BE HIM—Vikki Carr	Liberty	4
14	(13)	TALKING LOVE—Sean Dunphy and the Hoedowners	Pye	4
*15	(25)	I'LL NEVER FALL IN LOVE—Tom Jones	Decca	2
*16	(26)	DEATH OF A CLOWN—Dave Davies	Pye	2
17	(12)	CARRIE-ANNE—Hollies	Parlophone	9
18	(23)	FIVE LITTLE FINGERS—Frankie McBride and the Polka Dots	Emerald	4
19	(27)	THREE STEPS TO THE PHONE—Larry and the Mighty Avons	King	2
20	(14)	IRISH SOLDIER BOY—Pat Lynch and the Airchords	Pye	18
21	(17)	OLD MAID IN A GARRET—Sweeney's Men	Pye	13
22	(16)	OKAY—Dave Dee, Dozy, Beaky Mick & Tich	Fontana	4
23	(24)	THEN I KISSED HER—Beach Boys	Capitol	14
24	(—)	YOU ONLY LIVE TWICE—Nancy Sinatra	Reprise	1
25	(18)	SEVEN DRUNKEN NIGHTS—Dubliners	Major Minor	19
26	(21)	ENNISKILLEN DRAGOONS—The Ludlows	Pye	9
27	(28)	SILENCE IS GOLDEN—Tremeloes	C.B.S.	13
28	(22)	WATERLOO SUNSET—The Kinks	Pye	11
29	(20)	THE CURRAGH OF KILDARE—The Johnstons	Pye	11
30	(—)	YOU DIDN'T HAVE TO ME SO NICE—Strangers	Pye	1

* Denotes fastest mover of the week.

MIAMI

Ireland's chart topping all-time favourites . . .

THERE'S ALWAYS ME
Pye Piccadilly 7N 35154
I'M YOURS
Pye Piccadilly 7N 36185
FROM THE CANDY STORE
Pye Piccadilly 7N 35202
JUST FOR OLD TIME SAKE
Pye 7N 15229
ROUND AND AROUND
Pye 7N 15750
EVERY STEP OF THE WAY
Pye 7N 15855
I LEFT MY HEART IN SAN FRANCISCO
Pye 7N 15891
WISHING IT WAS YOU
Pye 7N 15977
BUCK'S POLKA
Pye 7N 17006
ONE KISS FOR OLD TIME'S SAKE
Pye 7N 17028
COME BACK TO STAY
Pye 7N 17063
DARLING I LOVE YOU
Pye 7N 17206
WHEN YOU CRY
Pye 7N 17253

Plus the MIAMI E.P.
NEP 24251
ROCK AND ROLL MUSIC
CANDY STORE
COME BACK TO STAY
GEORGIE PORGIE

ALL STILL AVAILABLE ON PYE

U.S.A.'s TOP TEN
10 LITTLE BIT OF SOUL—Music Explosion
9 PLEASANT VALLEY SUNDAY—Monkees
8 MERCY, MERCY, MERCY—Buckinghams
7 MERCY, MERCY, MERCY—Buckinghams
6 A WHITER SHADE OF PALE—Procol Harum
5 WINDY—Association
4 ALL YOU NEED IS LOVE—Beatles
3 I WAS MADE TO LOVE HER—Stevie Wonder
2 WHITE RABBIT—Jefferson Airplane
1 LIGHT MY FIRE—Doors

BRITAIN'S TOP TEN
10 SEE EMILY PLAY—Pink Floyd
9 DEATH OF A CLOWN—Dave Davies
8 UP, UP AND AWAY—Johnny Mann Singers
7 I'LL NEVER FALL IN LOVE AGAIN—Tom Jones
6 I WAS MADE TO LOVE HER—Stevie Wonder
5 ALTERNATE TITLE—Monkees
4 IT MUST BE HIM—Vikki Carr
3 ALL YOU NEED IS LOVE—Beatles
2 SAN FRANCISCO—Scott McKenzie
1 A WHITER SHADE OF PALE—Procol Harum

August 1967

This is a version of Ireland's Top Ten as featured every week in *Spotlight*. You can see from the listing that it was a really mixed bag. With the Beatles at number one, we then had Johnny Kelly and Joe Dolan. Followed by the Monkees and Englebert Humperdink. Next was Johnny McEvoy and Gregory keeping Pink Floyd and Procol Harum at bay, while Frankie McBride had 'Five Little Fingers' in both the Irish and English charts. Among the others that featured were the Dubliners, Ludlows and Sweeney's Men, along with the Beach Boys, Kinks, Tremeloes and Nancy Sinatra. Bands would have played most of the songs featured in the Top 20 in their repertoire.

Of course, we told them we were going to do a tour of Germany, we were a band and we were going to start in Hamburg. 'Have ye not heard of us?' We were going to be the next big thing! Anyway, they looked at us and one of them checked the passports.

'Oh, I see you're a band but I don't see any working visas here.'

'Ah, the visas, they are being organised by our manager and they are being sent out to us when they are ready you know, but we are starting anyway tomorrow night in Hamburg.'

'There is nothing I can do. You cannot get through here without visas and I would suggest that you go to Amsterdam, get your visas, come back and we will let you in.'

Jesus! What were we going to do now? We hadn't the time. We had intended to drive overnight hoping to arrive in Hamburg early the following day. We turned around and 'circled the wagon' for a little think on what we were going to do. We had to suss out a way of getting past this very grumpy German soldier.

Anyway, I don't know how, but we found out that shifts changed at 8pm and 8am so we reckoned that this guy would be going off shift at 8pm and wouldn't be back again until the following morning. We decided that we would go back to the nearest town which was about five miles away and stay there. We checked into a hotel with the intention of getting up around 5am and going through the checkpoint with a different story this time, before our 'friend' came back.

We had something to eat, went to bed, got up at the appointed hour, loaded up and headed off again for the checkpoint. We handed in the passports and said we were tourists going around Germany on a holiday.

'Right.' He stamped all the passports and sent us on our way.

We belted off up the road. Great, we had fooled the Germans, we were in and the visas would be along some time! A few miles later someone shouts, 'Oh, Jesus! The suits! Stop the van!'

'What about the suits?'

'I left them behind me. I took them out of the case because they were getting all crushed and I hung them up in the wardrobe and forgot to bring them this morning. They are still back in the hotel.'

Ah, Jesus Christ Almighty! Stick the van to the road, turn around and 20 minutes after entering Germany we were leaving Germany.

Your man looked at the passports. 'What is the situation here?'

'We forgot some stuff and we have to pick it up.'

So we booted back to the hotel, got the suits out of the wardrobe, loaded them up and belted back to the checkpoint. By now it was after 8am.

Pulling up at the crossing, who do we spy? Only our friend 'Happy Harry' himself; 'Günther-face' was back on duty.

'Good morning,' he says.

'Hello, we are going to Germany.'

'Yes, good, please show me your passports. What are you doing here in Germany?'

'We're tourists.'

'Hmm! Yes, I see you have already been here this morning and you went back out.'

'Oh yeah, we had to go back to the hotel … '

He flicked back through the pages to the day before. 'So, yesterday you were musicians and today you are tourists! Give me all the passports.' Thump, thump, thump he stamped every one of them 'get out now!' or words to that effect in German.

'Turn around your van, go and get your visas in Amsterdam and do not come back until you are legitimate.'

'Oh God, what are we doing to do?'

It was now 8.30am and we were due to be playing in the Star Club in Hamburg that night at 8pm, the opening night of our tour. Your man, Mr 'I Forgot The Suits', was staying very quiet in the back of the van. Even if we headed straight for Amsterdam and got the visas immediately, we wouldn't make it on time. What were we going to do? We first considered killing the guy who forgot the suits. The guy whose name we won't mention, for the moment!

Somebody had a bright idea. Get the map. We took out the map. The checkpoint we were at was a major checkpoint so we looked along the border for a smaller one. Sure enough, about 30 miles north, there was one. We decided to go up to this checkpoint, hopefully a smaller operation, and we would be well prepared and rehearsed. The girl singer was positioned in the front passenger seat with the passports. Her passport said she was a receptionist with no mention about being a musician. The idea was for her to smooth talk the guy, whoever he was going to be. Sure enough, we arrived up and it was just a 'hole in the wall' job, a one-man operation and he kind of leaning against the gate, like you would see in the pictures! Only one guy, we could be lucky! Hold your breath! We drove up.

The girl singer, all smiles, 'Hello, we're tourists going on a tour. Can we get through this way?'

Yes, yes, all nice and easy, showing her passport only.

'How many people?' says he.

She just had her own passport on top of the rest of them and she said, 'We have eight people, one, two, three, four, five, six, seven, eight passports and one, two, three, four, five, six, seven, eight people.' But she doesn't go so far as to give the passports to him.

And he waved us on, 'Okay, that is good. All is clear, you may go.'

We were through!

We're In!

So, boot to the floor, we're heading for Hamburg.

The Paddies had invaded Germany after avoiding two world wars and still we got in with no visas! The main thing was we had to get to the gig so we booted along. Pat McDonald from Derry was the driver. We used to call him 'Cab-happy' because he was happy only when he was driving the van.

Anyway, we arrived in Hamburg, a big city! 'Where's the hall?' we asked.

Pat decided to inquire around and to the first people we stopped, Pat said, in his lovely broken English, 'Hello, we musica, we play tonight in the Star Club, Hamburga.' Pat could speak all those languages, no more than a few more of us! 'We have to play tonight, very important we are there soon ...' and so on he goes.

The guy is eyeing Pat deadpan and letting him talk away. Eventually, he answered, 'Okay mate, you go down there to the traffic lights and swing a left ...'

He was English! We never let Pat live that one down!

I remembered the name of the place we were looking for was Harbour Strasse. It was obviously a street near the harbour but what we didn't realise was it was bang in the middle of the red light district. As we went up one street and down the next, panic was beginning to set in. It was after 6pm and we had no definite details as to when we were on.

You know when you want directions at home, the best place to ask is in a pub, so I ran into a pub and the people in it were all dolled up. 'We're playing in the Star tonight, does anyone know where it is? It's very urgent.'

I got the directions and went back out to the van saying, 'Jaysus, they're a very funny looking crowd in there, all very big, tall women.'

With that, one of the boys decided he wanted to have a look and he went in.

'No wonder they looked strange,' he said. 'It's a transvestite pub.'

Long Hours and Dry Throats

On we went to the Star Club. I can't remember our exact arrival but the scene was unreal. The club was open seven nights a week. Mid-season from 6pm until 4am, and in high season, which we played through on some of the nights, from 4pm until 6am.

Now, there would be five acts on, and we were only the second showband ever to appear. The first was a band from Dublin who had been there for a couple of months before that. They were hugely popular because up to then it had been all beat groups: four-piece, guitars and drums. There might be the odd keyboard player but there was no brass. These other guys were going a bomb because the style of the showband was so different. Later on, we were the first showband into Berlin!

Anyway, the deal was that you would play three hours but you only played one hour at a time. So, if you played from six to seven, as there were another three or four groups, you would go on again from eleven to twelve and then again from three to four. While we only played three hours, they were spread over a whole night which meant we couldn't go anywhere or if you did, you had to be back again very shortly.

There was great excitement and it was very different for us. There was a 'backline' there, which basically meant guitar amplifiers. I am not sure if there was a kit of drums or if we had our own drums. But you wouldn't have your own PA, there was a resident PA and you had to use that.

The club had a big stage, seated areas and a small dancefloor area. They sold liquor and beer and a lot of the punters stood around leaning on the stage drinking from beer bottles with plastic corks hooked on to them. As they were getting into the beat, they'd start banging the bottles on the stage.

After the first few nights a lot of the guys would get what was called 'Hamburg Throat'. I believe there are similar ones called 'Las Vegas Throat' or 'Nevada Throat'. This was mainly caused by the dry atmosphere in the club, but also because the house PA was different from our own. After maybe two or three nights, the singers would lose their voices but they just had to keep singing. So, everybody came out at the end of their tour with improved voices that had matured greatly because of work. We had to put up with a lot of drama during those few days before the voices came back again, but we just had to work through it.

'How do you sing without a voice?'

'I know, but some of them have been doing it for years.'

The first night was very strange, you would play for an hour, then break for three before going back on again for the second spot. I forget which slot we did but I remember we went down a storm. They were used to four-piece groups in jeans and casual gear playing rhythm and blues, whereas we wore suits, mohair suits. Also there were seven of us, a girl singer and a guy singer and we had a three-piece brass section. We played the Top 20 stuff; you know that type, the live jukebox stuff, and we were into 'doing the steps', the old showband choreography bit. But we really made an impact.

Other bands were possibly better musically than us but we had a package. Basically, we looked the part and we were doing everything from the charts like The Beatles, Elvis, Cliff Richard, The Bachelors, even numbers by The Clancy Brothers and we would do a few instrumentals like The Shadows and Herb Alpert. We were a breath of fresh air, just because the showband set up was so different. The versatility in style and variety of the programme always worked.

The Liver Birds

There were five acts on at any given time. You would do the hour and, invariably, bands would open up with a 'pet' tune. Nine times out of ten, that opening tune was Chuck Berry's 'Roll Over Beethoven'. From what I remember, they would alternate one band each week with most of them coming from the north of England, Liverpool in particular. We were always watching out for the new arrivals, checking out the opposition so to speak.

One week the new band happened to be an all-girl band called The Liver Birds. What a pleasant surprise, so we all hung around for their opening set, expecting something really different but guess what they opened with? 'Roll over Beethoven' and the rest of their set was pretty much along the same lines of the other groups, rhythm and blues all the way, played quite well though!

There was one guy in charge of the programme and he would schedule the line-up. The most popular bands would go on at the peak times so it would take a few nights for it to settle down. There would be a meeting every week and you would be given the slot you were on, but eventually we got moved up. The least popular acts would be on first and last, with one slot in the middle. The crowd kept moving, people would drift in for a couple of hours, then move on to another club and maybe come back again.

There were all sorts of guys and clubs. Gary Glitter was in another club called the Top Ten. He was known as Paul Raven then. One of the bands that was in our line-up was Freddie Starr and The Midnighters. I remember the locals weren't wearing him at all, he was nearly a 'has-been', a spent force in Liverpool and I remember at one of the meetings he was complaining about how he was getting the bad slots. Even at home he was considered to be over the hill. About six months after going back to England, his band split up and he went solo. We met him again when we lived in London. He spotted our van and drove up in an E-type Jag. He had become a solo comedian and his career had taken off.

A major happening took place on the last Saturday of every month. Polygram Records would come in and record the whole night; good, bad and ugly, everybody was recorded so everybody was on file. There would be a changeover at the end of the month, some band would be going back to England but the drummer might want to stay on, and in another club somebody else from a band might want to stay on. Very often, a new band would be formed this way.

I remember one particular occasion, two guys out of two bands in our club and another guy who was in another band in a different club wanted to stay on so they were let do the early work slots in order to give them a chance to build up their programme. Many a good band started this way and it was in fact how Rory Gallagher started to work as a three-piece. He was out there with a showband called The Impact. I had met them in London when I was with The Millionaires and we were both staying in a small hotel that catered for musicians. The one thing we had in common was that we had both been to Germany, so we talked a lot about that. He was really switched on with the German thing. While I liked it for the experience, it wasn't really a showband scene. But I remember him telling me that he was going to go back on a tour with the band and then he was going to stay there. When The Impact's stint finished, Rory stayed on working as a three-piece. That time gave him the initial feel for the blues group that would eventually become Taste. The rest, as they say, is history. If you go back even further, you could almost say that Rory started out in music as a direct result of the showbands. Read on.

When the manager of The Royal Showband, TJ Byrne,

spotted the latest Fender Stratocaster guitar on display in Crowley's of Cork he was convinced it would add greatly to the band's image. He was so impressed with the new model that he persuaded the band's guitarist, Jim Conlon, to trade in his already good Fender for this latest colourful model. As soon as the traded second-hand Fender, 'in mint condition', was put on display in Crowley's it was spotted by a young rocker who was into the blues and rock 'n' roll. After trying it out in the shop, this lad brought his mother along to view the 'magic musical machine' in the hope of convincing her to buy it for him. After some financial discussions with the shop manager, a suitable payment structure was agreed which resulted in a very excited young rocker leaving the shop with a guitar that was to become his constant companion as he toured the world for the next 25 years. Alongside his Vox AC30 amp, this Fender 'Strat' was to play a major role in the highly successful career of one Rory Gallagher.

Going back to our tour of Germany, after we finished our first week in Hamburg we packed up and flew to the next venue which was Berlin. You would arrive in the early afternoon, get to the club, set up and play that night. There would be no night off to travel or anything like that, it was tough work.

I liked Berlin. There were a lot of American GIs so our programme went down a storm. We had real variety; we would do a lot of American stuff whereas the British groups would do rhythm and blues. They were very good at it but it was just the one style. We had a girl singer and we would do ballads, The Bachelors and Bobby Darin stuff. Also, because we had brass and piano, we would go in and jam with the other acts and this turned into quite a nice thing.

If we were going on at midnight, we would be ready at that time and the guy who was finishing up, in particular Lee Curtis who used to do quite a lot of Ray Charles material, would invite us on to play with him for the last song. Then he would mosey off and we would take it from there. But, especially on the night of the recording in Hamburg, we would be invited to play with a couple of acts just to beef up the performance. Our piano guy played with two or three of them and our trumpet and sax appeared with a few different acts. I remember seeing an album one time with a photograph on the back of it, and there was our tenor player rocking away with Lee Curtis, Beryl Marsden and some other would-be star who we have never heard of since! But it was very, very exciting.

Kiel and the English £5 Note

To break up our time in Berlin, we did a short stint in Kiel. We stayed in the Harbour Port area which was very battered from the war. Down around the docks you could see the walls were all bullet-ridden and the people were very cold. They treated us all as English and we were the enemy. This was 1964, less than 20 years after the war ended.

One time, we were going to visit the Zoo with some of the guys out of one of the other bands, I think it was Freddie Starr and The Midnighters. Anyway, there was a guy selling papers and one of the English lads went up and asked for directions. Your man wouldn't talk to him at all, muttering things like 'British scum, British pigs' and so on. Obviously my mate took umbrage so I went up to the paper seller and said, 'I'm not English, I'm Irish.'

So he said to me, 'Okay, my friend.' And he proceeded to give me the directions. Obviously, my mate was coming with me but he just wouldn't talk to him at all. We noticed also that when you would go into restaurants, you would ask for the menu and enquire if they spoke English?

'No, no we don't speak English.'

As I said, they were very, very cold. I suppose they had memories but they just didn't want to know us.

Breakfast in Kiel

The money we were getting was brutal but it didn't really matter. The experience was well worth it and we would have nearly cycled out to the place. I was a young fellow, 17 or 18 years of age, and it was like going to the moon.

Anyway, with eight of us in the band we had to try and budget the cash. We were staying in this type of a Bed & Breakfast where you had to pay extra for breakfast when you came down. So there was a bit of 'hanging around'!

'Are you going down for breakfast?'

'No, I'm going to wait for a while.'

'Are you going down for breakfast?'

'No, I'll go down later on.'

Next thing, somebody said, 'You wouldn't have a loan of a few marks, would ye?'

'No, I haven't. I was going to ask you for a loan.'

It turned out that nobody had money; everyone was broke, so that's why nobody was rushing down to breakfast! Pat was the only one with money, he was the sax man and always a good steady guy. All he had though was an English fiver, so we worked out a plan. We would go down, order the normal breakfast, eat it and Pat would pay for the lot with his English fiver. If there was a problem, well we had the breakfast eaten anyway! This was on a Thursday and we wouldn't get paid until Friday.

Down we went and guess what, the regular breakfast which we were used to ordering, was off the menu! No way, they didn't speak English and weren't very helpful at all. So now, what were we doing to do? So Pat 'Onions' Green, the singer, decided he would go into the kitchen and have a look to see if he could recognise anything that they could cook for us. He spots something like streaky bacon and explains to the girl, 'Cut this up and that will do the job grand.'

Sure enough, we were sitting down and out comes the breakfast so we wired into it. Then Betty, the other singer, said, 'This is raw, I can't eat this.'

There were a few remarks like, 'Jaysus! If she was hungry, she'd eat it.' But then we copped on, it was raw; they hadn't cooked it at all. So back in again, we called over the girl but no, she couldn't understand. So 'Onions' goes back into the kitchen again bringing Betty with him, got out a pan and showed them. You put the pan on the cooker, heat it up, put streaky rashers on the pan and you fry them. Eventually we got our breakfast. When it was all eaten anyway, raw and cooked, the whole shebang, the bill arrived. Pat produced his lovely English fiver, which didn't get a great welcome from them, but sure we didn't give a damn, we had the grub eaten by then. Anyway, they had to take the fiver.

One exciting breakfast later, we head off for the day to go sightseeing, hoping we wouldn't get shot or poisoned.

Berlin

During our two weeks in Berlin, we had a great time. The American GIs, they were all over us; you know the Americans! This guy befriended us and he became 'our pal, our roadie' and so he wanted to show us all over the place, this guy knew everything! So we said all right, we would like to see Checkpoint Charlie and the Wall and all this stuff. Anyway, we arrived up at Checkpoint Charlie where the late President Kennedy had been sometime in the previous 12 months or so. They had brought him to Checkpoint Charlie and built this platform so that he could look over the wall into 'no man's land' on the other side, but that little platform was still there and I have photographs to prove it! Every tourist went up and looked over. It was harrowing but interesting and thankfully it's now all gone.

This GI scout was taking us everywhere on the train. The system, it was both underground and overground, ran through the whole of Berlin. We were in West Berlin and East Berlin was where the Russians were. The train originated from East Berlin as the staff were East Berliners and they would go out across the border into West Berlin and then the service would go right around the circle and back into East Berlin. We wondered how come the boys didn't scarper off the train, the drivers and conductors and all that. We were told they were hand-picked; it was all family men that drove the trains. If they had young single people on it, they would all take off when they got to the West. We could see them, their faces were so sad looking, expressionless, grey, like their uniforms. It was very sad really, but this was their job going around on the trains.

But anyway, the 'Yankee-doodle' was bringing us on the tour and giving us a commentary, 'This is such and such and this is such and such.'

Of course, we wanted to go as near as possible to the Wall and then he said, 'Now in the distance you can see the Berlin Wall.'

Then next stop and the next stop, we were beside the Berlin Wall and next stop, we were beyond the Wall, looking back at it! I remember seeing Russian soldiers and women doing manual labour, digging with picks and shovels. So, we get off at the next stop and I said to your man, 'Should we be in here? We have no visas or anything.'

He said it was fine, everything would be okay. He knew everything of course, you know the type, but we soon found out. We got off and we were going down steps to go out of the station and next thing we spotted these soldiers with guns. I said, 'Jesus, I'm not going down there.'

We turned and got back on the train. If we had gone down without proper visas, we would have been arrested and this did happen to one group, The Undertakers from Liverpool. They were thrown into jail and were there for three weeks before the Consulate eventually got them out. It was just a case of their being in a place they had no right to be in. We were nearly on another type of a holiday!

You had no problem getting into Berlin; everyone could get in there without being checked, there was never an issue. I think we were a good four weeks into the tour at this stage and our visas still hadn't arrived and we were due to leave Berlin. Now, the procedure was that every person leaving Berlin was checked, whether you were going by train, plane, bus or whatever. The idea was to capture anyone who might have escaped from the East and was trying to get out of Berlin itself.

We finished our gig on the Saturday night, packed up everything and headed to the airport to fly back to Hamburg. We had all the gear at the airport and you know the usual, check in, three fellows minding the gear while the others went for something to eat, Then they would come back and the others could go but, as normal, the first gang would 'forget' to come back and the rest of us would be left minding the gear. They eventually came back and I said, 'I have to get something to eat.' And I go running up to get something.

I shouted back to the lads, 'Start bringing over the stuff and check it in. I'll be back in a few minutes.'

So, sure enough, there was a panic. 'Oh! We're in trouble, major trouble. We're not being let out of Berlin, because we have no visas, we're going to be hanged at dawn!'

Back up to the official and sure enough, we're not getting out and we due to fly in a half hour!

I don't remember what was and wasn't said, but somehow we got through and onto the plane. The promoters who were running the gig laid on a big farewell and they had a lovely little souvenir for us. It seems that one of the symbols of Berlin is a little teddy bear and, as we got up to the steps to the plane, there was a lady from the club standing there presenting us with these lovely little teddy bears. I don't know where the bear is now but all I remember was as soon as I got to the steps of the plane, I was no more interested in a teddy bear, I just wanted to get on the plane and get the hell out of Berlin in case we might meet our American 'tour guide' again.

Black Bombers

We arrived back in Hamburg, very tight for time, and got from the airport to the Star Club to do our gig. We hadn't been to bed at all the night before because when we finished the gig we travelled. We just went in and played our first slot and then back into the band room afterwards. There was all kinds of stuff lying around in there as you can imagine with four or five bands coming and going. We literally came off stage, into the band room, lay down and fell asleep knowing somebody would wake us when our next slot came up. We were wrecked. I dozed off with my head on a guitar case, I could sleep anywhere. But I remember at one stage two guys whispering and one guy lifting up my head trying not to wake me, to get out his guitar case. Obviously he was going to play next and he was putting back in another case, all the time trying not to wake me.

'The poor devils, they must be wrecked.'

Eventually we woke and were getting ready for the gig and I remember a guy coming over and saying, 'Hey guys, you need some help? No need to be torturing yourselves like this. Here take a few of these little things and they will get you through the night.'

They could have been purple hearts or black bombers but they were drugs anyway. I said, 'No thanks, I'm a pioneer.'

And this was 1964, some guys think they invented all that kind of stuff.

Maybe that was the 'drugs' part of 'sex, drugs and rock and roll'. The 'rock and roll' bit I remember; as for the rest of it, well, as the saying goes, 'If you remember the Sixties, then you weren't even there!'

Finally, the tour was finished and it was time to head on back to dear old England.

We drove back through Germany, Holland and Belgium without a problem. I'd say they were glad to be rid of us! We then travelled by boat and I remember seeing the white cliffs as we approached Dover and, while they weren't quite as white as I expected them to be, it was still nice to see them!

We arrived in England and headed up towards London, stopping at a transport café for a big greasy fry, it was lovely. I spent ages looking over the jukebox and the first song I put on was Manfred Mann's 'Doo Wah Diddy'. It was number one at the time and we digging into this big greasy fry. We knew we were back in England.

Of course, on the way back on the boat I feel asleep and got all sunburned on one side of me. I was pure red on one side and pure white on the other, so I was two-tone when I got back. We went straight down to Selmer's in Charing Cross Road; it was a big music shop and we were happy to have people talking English to us again! We knew a lot of the musicians from resident bands who worked in music shops and a sax player that I knew from one of the clubs, was working in this shop. He came up to me and said, 'What happened you? What happened your boat race?'

Anyway, we were back in Blighty and half-baked. That was the end of the German tour. Don't mention the visas or the war. What war?

Styles of the Sixties
As a child or product of the Sixties, I've always considered myself very fortunate to have been of that generation, as this enabled

me to participate in the pop and fashion revolution of that era. While we found ourselves being guided out of the grey and gloomy Fifties by de Valera and the tweed jacket brigade with the leather patches on the elbows, along came Bill Haley, Elvis and Adam Faith to propel us into the swinging Sixties with their drainpipe trousers, blue suede shoes and DA hairstyles.

The Beatles and The Rolling Stones not only changed the style of music of the time but also had a major impact on the fashion of the day. With their mop-top hairstyles, Beatle boots and collarless jackets, along with those brilliant black polo neck jumpers, sure the ladies were lucky to get a look in at all.

Not to be outdone however, the female of the species followed in the footsteps of trendsetters like Mary Quant, Twiggy and Sandie Shaw as they pranced along Portobello Road on their way to Chelsea, Carnaby Street and Grafton Street to join in the flower power movement with the multi-coloured, psychedelic, peace-loving hippies of London and Dublin. They had the heads twisted off us poor unfortunate young lads as we tried our best to keep our sanity amidst the rapidly decreasing length of the mini-skirt.

And now as I struggle to regain my composure, I will reveal what my favourite fashion item of the Sixties was. The black polo neck jumper. I still have mine.

Eight
The Business

Manager's Database

In August 1968, I returned to Galway to get married and join forces with The Raindrops, and fortunately one of those unions was successful! On returning from a short tour of England in October of that year, The Raindrops were informed by their manager that, due to pressure of other business, he could no longer look after our affairs. So, I found myself propelled into the position of player/manager. I remember saying at the time that the reality was there was only one way we could go and that was up, because we only had three dates in the diary. Things looked very bleak indeed as we headed into the winter. We had two chances, slim and none. Option one, give it a go and see what happens. If it isn't working after a few months then we pack it in, split up and go our separate ways. Glad to report that option two worked out – survival. We made it through that lean winter and went on to get another few years out of The

Raindrops before revamping and relaunching ourselves as The Big Time in 1975.

In an effort to get a handle on the management side of things, I started to compile a listing of halls and marquees and proceeded to buy a group of provincial papers for the best part of a year. At the end of this little marketing exercise I had a list of every venue in the various regions, what particular nights they operated and the type or standard of band they used on different nights. As the carnival season ran from Easter to the end of September, I was able to compile a list of the location and date of each carnival.

While I worked on my list, I set off in my little Volkswagen Beetle on a nationwide tour, up and down the highways and byways of Ireland until I had covered almost every county. I must have called to every hall owner and carnival secretary's house in the country with my bundle of photographs and posters. Whenever I hear politicians talking about canvassing the country for Senate seats I know exactly what they're talking about. Hunting down the carnival committees was great craic. In lots of cases the secretary would be a different person each year and you'd arrive in a place not having a clue who you were looking for. This was never a problem really, because all you had to do was head straight for the local priest, guard or teacher and you were put on the right track. On one occasion, I was directed to a farmhouse where the secretary lived only then to be told he was down the fields ploughing. No problem to me, I headed off down the fields following the sound of the tractor and soon located him. We chatted away for a while, with him above on the tractor and, after twenty minutes or so, I was on my merry way having secured a booking for a Friday night in Kilmurray McMahon carnival in the lovely County Clare, thanks to Mr Halloran. Clare was a great county for halls and marquees.

Ennis, Kilrush, Killaloe and Kilkee, Kilmurray McMahon, Kilmaley, Kilmihil, Kildysart, Kilkishen. Jaysus, a fella would be killed out touring County Clare alone.

Those were the days of the phone box where you had to book your trunk calls by calling the exchange and then waiting 15 to 30 minutes for the operator to call you back. You were then instructed to 'insert your money and press button "A" please', while you waited to be told, 'you're through now,' and later, 'your three minutes are up so finish up now, please.'

Can you imagine telling today's generation to wait for 15 minutes and finish after three minutes? No such luxuries as laptops or mobile phones in those days.

Ye're Too Loud, Ye're Too Dear, Ye've No Accordion and Ye Won't Be Back!

Of course, there was often the hard luck story at the end of the night; things were never great in the old 'biscuit tin' school of economics department!

'Twas a bad night,' mumbled the promoter as he rattled the biscuit tin when I entered the box office.

'Judging by the look on your face,' says I to myself, 'I have a feeling it's gonna get worse,' as I prepared for the post mortem, the 'where did it all go wrong lads?'

'Sure have a look in the tin there and see for yourself. By the time I have paid for the hall, the *Tribune*, doormen, cloakroom and mineral bar staff, the meal for the band and the car park attendant, I'll have damn all left to pay ye.' Everyone seemed to get paid before the band, and we thinking we were the main event.

'Hmm, what do ye mean ye can't give us a cut?'

'Ye say you want yere full fee, is it? Sure we're trying to develop a pitch and dressing-rooms here and we're hoping to put a roof on the school hall. There was a great band here last week and there was eight of them in it and they weren't as dear as ye crowd; sure I remember getting ye last year for £50.'

'Yeah,' says one of our lads, 'and I remember getting a gallon of petrol last year for 50p, it is now 80p.'

'That's my wages you have in your paw there,' said a pleading bandleader when trying to collect his reasonable fee of £100 for a seven-piece band.

The promoter stopped when he had counted out £80 and he quipped, 'Have ya not enough yet?'

I suppose one of the advantages of the 'one nighters' was that at least you got your money on the night; there was no such thing as the 30 days credit, even if you were docked 20 per cent. Within an hour of the dance finishing, you were driving out the road with your money in your pocket – whatever it was, that's what you got and that's all you were going to get. Hopefully it would be cash so you could divide it up on the spot in whatever way was required. Bands were always wary of the dreaded 'Gregory Peck' or 'chicken's neck'.

'Will you rifle range a chicken's neck?'

'How can we rifle range a chicken's neck at this hour of the night? I hope it's not a "Dunlop".'

Running a Dance

I would like to spend a little time looking at the various activities involved in organising a dance or a public function. There are many crucial elements to it but I suppose the main elements would be the promoter who would supply the venue and the band who supplied the music. But there was more to it than that. There were lots of different elements when you were 'running the dance' as the term would have been. When I think back to those early days, the dance played a big role in the social aspect of life as dancing was the main opportunity for the 'boy meets girl' situation. I would say that nine times out of ten, that's where most couples met. You could meet somebody at the dance, see them home and then make a date for the following week. Maybe go to the cinema together and then the next dance and hopefully it would build from there. In some cases it didn't work, but generally speaking that's how it went.

So, to the process and procedures of running a dance. If the promoter owned the ballroom or the hall, they would be running at least one dance a week, in some cases two. Their main function would be to provide the venue and advertising for the dance. If it were a weekly occurrence, they would have their usual slot in the local paper with their regular weekly advertisement containing the name of the band and any other special things. They would then have posters around the town and provide the staff for the door, cloakroom, tearoom and mineral bar.

Very definitely there was no 'bar' situation as there were no licensed premises in the ballrooms until much later on when the showband scene was nearly dead. The sale of liquor was introduced through ballrooms being attached to hotels and covered by the hotel licence. Prior to this, 99 per cent of ballrooms were 'dry'.

If there were two venues in a bigger town, they obviously had to watch that there were no clashes. For instance, if there was a showband playing at one venue, then they would run a céilí in the other. So, the promoter provided the venue, all administration and advertising, and also the band's fee plus a meal.

The band consisted of six to eight members and a manager. The fee had to cover payment to the band members, provision of instruments and equipment, transport to take them to and from the venue and their promotional material such as posters and photographs. As time went on, the band might start to record. All that had to come out of the band's takings. The bigger bands would command bigger fees and better conditions. For instance, they could get a deal of 50/50 of the takings with a guarantee of say £100 to £200 minimum. If the takings were £500 they would get £250. On the other hand, if the takings were only £100 they would still get their guaranteed amount. To get those conditions, you had to be pretty popular and pretty confident of drawing a good crowd. Really, it was only the top five or ten bands that could do this. In most cases, it was a straight fee. In the early and late 1960s, the entrance charge to a dance could be 5 or 10 'bob' (shillings equal to 35 to 65 cent each), depending on the time and the grade of band. Sunday night was popular for dancing so a 'middle of the road' band would do, but on a Thursday night, which wasn't so popular, that's when you would have the bigger band, one of the top 10 or 20 bands.

The neighbouring towns would be watching each other to keep a close eye on the opposition. If a particular band played in a locality twenty miles away on a Thursday night, there wasn't much point in you having them the following Sunday night. It might happen by accident every so often but it was a rare occurrence. This was the commercial ballroom. The same applied if it was a parochial hall run by a priest or a committee. They would have to book the band and watch out for the advertising.

If a club or society wanted to run a dance, they would have to hire the hall for a night and take responsibility for hiring the band, looking after the advertising and applying for a dance licence. If there were visiting acts in from the UK you would often see, 'By kind permission of the IFM' which stood for Irish Federation of Musicians. That was the union for musicians and part of the agreement would be that they would use local lads as support. Generally, this was used as an opportunity by both the ballroom proprietor to get a cheaper band at a smaller fee, and if there was a band who wanted to get in there, it was an opportunity for them to go in and show their talents. This was a kind of 'loss leader' situation, playing support to the bigger band and hoping that the proprietor would like you and bring you back at a later date on your own strength.

Sometimes the band would actually be the promoter, by that I mean the band would hire the venue and run the dance. In this case, they would be liable for all the administration but generally they would use the same people as usual. They would just pay a fee and all the extra work would be included in the rental.

Generally, bands would only do this if they happened to be free on a Thursday or Friday night. Not too often was there a killing made in this situation. It didn't look too good or 'healthy' if a band had to be hiring a hall themselves, but sometimes it worked out to their advantage. However, in most cases the promoter looked after the venue and all the logistics which went with that, and the band provided the entertainment and, hopefully, got a fee accordingly.

The Tricks of The Trade
Publicity, Records, Marketing, Masterstrokes and Spoofers

Just like in any business, marketing played a major role in the entertainment business, and from day one the showband scene was notorious for the hyping and the spoofing of whatever gimmick or publicity stunt you could come up with. The motto being just push yourself up another rung of the ladder and try and get ahead of the posse and then stay ahead. Everything was 'open-season' and there were some unique schemes. Initially there were little handout photographs and then posters. Then later there were the posters with a photograph on them. Any old excuse was used to get coverage in the local press; some of them as trivial as the introduction of an organ or keyboard to the band's line-up.

The very first 'electronic keyboard' was the clavoline organ. You might remember the Del Shannon song called 'Runaway' with this squeaky sound on the instrumental solo. That was played on a clavoline organ. The bands would have it in their quotes, 'The dynamic Wondertones featuring the clavoline organ. Sunday night fee for band £25; with clavoline organ £28.'

Along with the electric guitar, it was an extra special feature but the sound of the yoke would make your ears bleed. Somebody once described it as a 'wasp in a bottle' but it was one of the first gimmicks. I remember another classic blurb, a band with seven musicians with lovely suits in a specially heated van so that when they arrived at a venue they would be ready to put on a scintillating performance. Also, there was the proviso that if a hot meal was supplied, the band would be able to perform to a higher level. Bands would have fliers out, a publicity sheet describing them as 'the rage of the West' or 'the stars of the South', anything at all. Sometimes they would spoof about recordings and all sorts of non-existent stuff, 'young, versatile, punctual', 'speciality – the top of the pops' or 'strict tempo music', and 'ability to cater for all tastes'.

It really was a case of paper never refusing ink; who was ever going to check what they printed anyway? Any band could tip themselves for the top or state they were the greatest thing since sliced bread. You could be tipped for the top by your mother or your mates. You could say that you were the next big rage, it never had to be clarified. It was light-hearted and it looked good on paper.

Lists of Dates in the Evening Papers
As bands began to advertise in the papers they would put in a 'diary' and very often the diary was spoofed up to make it look as if you would be playing four or five nights a week. If there was a free night, it didn't look good so you would put in 'playing Friday night Ballycastle' without clarifying which one as there are numerous towns called Ballycastle. Then if you met someone

who said, 'I thought I saw The Freshmen advertised to play in Ballycastle on Friday. How come you're playing there too?'

You could reply like a shot, 'Ah, sure they're in Ballycastle in Antrim. We're in Ballycastle in Mayo.'

The same with Milltown, there are about five Milltowns and you never specified which one. It could be Milltown near Tuam or Milltown in Clare. It also worked with Corofin and Newport.

Another great one was when the bands started sponsoring their own radio programmes to promote their dancing diaries. Whenever they had a slack week it was very easy to pad it with a few spoof dates like 'Tuesday night – student dance, Belfast'. Now, Belfast is a big place!

Another one was 'Friday night – recording'. I remember one band publishing a witty gig list along the lines of:

Thursday night – playing Pavilion, Omagh

Friday night – playing Plaza, Tipperary

Saturday night – playing Stella, Limerick

Sunday night – playing Stardust, Cork

Monday night – playing Darts, The King's Head

Excuses

For a long while, Sunday was the big night and any band worth their salt had to play. It was a major problem and a big dent in the ego if you weren't. So, if you happened to be free on a Sunday night you could not be seen around the town. In our neck of the woods you wouldn't be even allowed go to the cinema because you might be spotted and the comment would be, 'Ye're not playing tonight then!'

The trick was that if you wanted to go out anywhere you

would have to go to the next town and in our case, as we were based in Tuam, we had to go to Galway to the pictures. We nearly had to wear sunglasses when we were going out, it was that bad. Sometimes the band would actually drive out of the town around teatime and maybe go to Galway or some other big town pretending we were playing, but the main thing was to be seen leaving.

I mentioned earlier that the worst thing that could happen was to be seen not playing on the 'popular' nights. However, we had all these pre-arranged excuses if you were unlucky enough to meet the observant wiseguy with the greeting, 'Ye're not playing tonight lads, what's the problem?'

'Oh, the priest died and the dance had to be cancelled.'

Another one was, 'The hall was burned down, so the dance had to be called off.'

Another trick was that if you were short of one member of the band you would get a guy to stand in and hang a rhythm guitar around his neck, but you wouldn't plug it in. The lead would be brought around the back of the stage and tied to the leg of the drummer's chair and the stand-in would then 'throw the shapes'. Some of the promoters weren't behind the door either when it came to publicity tricks. There was a hall in north Mayo which was attached to the local bar. There were a few other halls quite nearby and the competition was fierce. The patrons would drive up and park outside listening to whatever band was playing and if they didn't like them, they would move on to the next hall. Sometimes, they would even approach the door in an effort to have a look to see if there were many patrons inside. The doormen however, would not allow anybody to look in and they would be cued to applaud after every tune and we, the band, were instructed that after playing a couple of tunes we were to announce, 'That will be all for now, ladies and gentlemen, your next dance please,' or, 'This time, we continue dancing with ...'

At this stage, there may not be anybody in the hall but to those in the cars it sounded as if it was all action inside.

Reaching for the Stars

The quest for stardom was unreal. How can we move up to the next rung of the ladder? There was every sort of gimmick like changing the name of the band every so often, get new suits, get a new singer and put him out front. During Lent the pressure would really be on because the season started on Easter Sunday with the marquees opening up. During Holy Week there would be a major revamp and, because there were no gigs, it was the perfect time for rehearsing and getting organised with the new act.

With regard to changing of the name, there was a guy from Armagh called Hughie Traynor who had a band, and things were not going too well so he decided to change the name of the band. They were called Hughie Traynor and his Dance Band or some such name. At the time, the trend was for such names as The Royal Showband or The Capitol Showband. As they were from Armagh, the cathedral city, some genius had this brilliant idea, 'Let's call ourselves The Cathedral Showband.'

They got handouts printed with a photograph of the cathedral with one main steeple in the centre at the top and five or six mini-steeples around it with an individual head and shoulders circular photograph of each member of the band on the mini-steeples with the bould Hughie on his own on the main steeple. So there they were, 'The Cathedral Showband – the boys from the County Armagh'.

There was another band from the North who were resident in Romano's in Belfast and they were at it for years. They were great singers and musicians, almost too good, but people were getting too familiar with them, as they were seeing them every week. So they decided to change the name of the band to The Silhouettes. That was all right but they then decided to wear black masks with numbers on them. The bandleader would announce, 'Now we have number four who is going to sing the latest number by Tom Jones,' or, 'This time we feature number five who will play a guitar solo.'

Bear in mind, this band was based in Belfast and here they were all wearing these black balaclava type hoods with numbers on them. Well, hello like? I should mention that this was around 1967. Somehow I imagine that by the time of the outbreak of the 'Troubles' in 1969 they had considered changing their name and routine again.

Any idea was worth a try, no matter how ridiculous it seemed. I even remember some lads dressing up as Indians! Feathers, warpaint, the lot, and guess what, it worked a treat! They got a good 30 years work out of it, and they're still at it.

Holy Week, Herald Awards and Special Trains
Holy Week was the time for the big rehearsals, getting ready for the season, the carnivals and maybe the big breakthrough. New season, new name, new promotions, new jackets, new singer and new hope; maybe this time. This could be our time!

'If we could only have a hit record we would be made up. We

could get the new posters. Maybe that's it, let's get stickers, headbands, calendars, flashy suits, vans.' Louis Copeland looked after the top bands with the classier stuff but he was a bit on the dear side for us lower division bands. Jas Fagan would have catered for most of the bands, a big advantage being the fact that he played trombone with The Cadets so he had a real feel for what the bands needed.

Later on, there were things like the 'Herald Awards' – the Evening Herald and then the Tuam Herald. A lot of guys got writer's cramp writing in about their 'favourite band'. 'We love the Wannabees.' It can be hard work hyping yourself anonymously.

Certain bands would run trains to their gigs and one very well known one was the 'Johnny Flynn Special'. Johnny Flynn's band was very big in the North and at one time they were playing in Blackrock outside Dundalk and a special trainload of fans travelled down from Belfast. Years later The Royal Blues used that idea when playing in Tuam. They were trying to come up with a gimmick and Miko Kelly, the ballroom manager, suggested the idea of running a special train from Claremorris. It was given such hype in the local press that the hall was jammed, not with people who came on the train from Claremorris, but with the hundreds who came in cars to see the crowds who were going to be there. In fact, very few came on the special train.

Another publicity story was about John Keogh and the Greenbeats from Dublin. They came to play in Galway in the new Skyline at Merlin Park. Unfortunately, there was a row in the crowd which spilled up on to the stage and some of the band's gear was knocked over. They got major publicity in the national press about this. I remember talking to one of the guys in the band later and saying that their gear must have been wrecked. He told me that the only thing that was broken was a valve in the amplifier worth about £5, but they got thousands of pounds worth of publicity out of the incident.

Splits, Revamps and Gimmick Names

Up to the mid 1960s most bands were paid a weekly wage by the leader until some of the newly formed outfits started to introduce the co-op system. When word of this got around it became a cause of unrest in some of the 'wages' bands. I can recall the comments, 'He's making a fortune out of our talents,' and the banner headlines, 'Band Split Over Artistic Differences'. We all knew the main reason for most of the break-ups was money of course. It was always a big deal when a band would split.

Even the break-up of a band could be turned into an opportunity and used as a gimmick for publicity. For the bigger bands, it was big stuff. For instance in the early 1960s some of Johnny Flynn's band members left to form The Ohio. That was a major news story but it also created new interest in both bands: people were watching out for the new band and also the fresh faces in Johnny Flynn's outfit, wondering how were they going to cope.

In most cases, both bands went on to do big business and of course the splits created big publicity. Someone had a theory, if you cut a garden worm in two, both halves of the worm will take off in two different directions, so from having just one worm you now had two worms. That's all very well, but what about the many small worms already in the field! All we saw was more worms creating more opposition for us.

Some bands were musically very good but, for whatever reason, things never clicked for them. A classic case was The Casino, the musician's favourite band. They were great musicians, great brass players, great singers and, although they played all the top venues, they just didn't get the recognition they deserved. The lads in the band realised this and came up with the idea of The Indians, a masterstroke. They dressed up accordingly and became huge. But again, full marks to the guys who were smart enough to twig that if they were to change the name, use a gimmick and a different programme, they must take it seriously to make it work. So, just as they did in The Casino, they approached things professionally. Their programme was always well thought out and well presented, plus they had a very good marketing manager so they were successful. So sometimes a change, if well managed, will work.

In the meantime, a lot of guys were watching from the sidelines taking note of what was going on. Suddenly a crowd of 'yellow packs' appeared on the scene, The Cowboys, The Monkeys (an Irish band as opposed to the American Sixties boyband), The Zulus and The Apaches. You always had to be ready for the 'me too brigade' latching on to the latest gimmick. For instance, when The Cadets were seen to be doing well, up sprang The Mounties and The Marines. There was always someone watching who would come up with a copycat idea, almost a carbon copy of someone else's.

Another angle was to latch on to a current topic like the space race which spawned a few gems like The Sputnicks and The Skyrockets. But surely the sickest of all time must have been The Assassins who were launched around the time of President Kennedy's death.

Stars of Stage, Screen, Radio and TV

With the arrival of television in the early 1960s there was a show called The Showband Show. To succeed in getting an appearance on that show was a massive boost. It really was just the bigger bands that got on, but it was a live show so you had to be fairly confident at what you were doing and some of the bands were caught out. They might have been great in a ballroom but, musically, they may not have been as tight as they would have liked; different bands had different talents. Some of the tightest bands, featuring the better musicians, may not have doing the business in the ballrooms but would have sounded great on TV and vice versa. There was also a debate about whether it was worth taking the chance to go on. Anyway, it was great publicity and fantastic to see bands on television. The sound balance always left a lot to be desired technically, but we were all learning about this new fangled thing called 'live TV'.

We took the chance and went on. The Millionaires appeared on The Showband Show in January 1966 and we played a few numbers, among them Herb Alpert's 'Spanish Flea' and Len Barry's 'One, Two, Three'. I think we did all right, nobody froze anyway!

Recording

During the Big Band era the vocalist would sit at the side of the stage waiting for the call from the band leader to sing maybe just three or four songs per hour. This was the norm at that time. Even when singers like Frank Sinatra recorded with The Tommy Dorsey Orchestra or Ross McManus with Joe Loss, the rule was they could only sing the middle section with the band playing the first and last sections. This was all to change however, as Sinatra soon became the first pin-up boy for the 'bobby socks brigade'. As this trend continued across the US and the UK it was only a matter of time before it would catch on here as well.

So, when bands started to record it brought some major changes to the industry. For starters, their records could be heard on national radio which gave them a high profile and helped them get bookings all over the country. It also meant that the featured vocalist would get extra publicity and in time this would cause its own problems. Some of the backing musicians started to resent the fact that your man was 'getting all the glory', while the band leader became worried that his frontman might get too big for his boots, start looking for more money or, worse still, get poached by the opposition. Eventually this did begin to happen, but in the meantime the fashion of billing became Dickie and the Miami, Butch and the Capitol, Eileen Reid and the Cadets.

When the bands started recording, the publicity machine went to a new level altogether. Records were a great vehicle for publicity, a marketing person's delight. It presented a great opportunity for write-ups, posters and interviews. It certainly was not about record sales as the market in Ireland was so small. The big attraction for bands to record was the amount of national exposure it offered through airplay. One spin on national radio was equal to pages of regional newspapers. The band's name was heard all over the country. If your record was lucky enough to get a dozen or so airplays then you could be sure you had a hit on your hands.

One of the most successful records from the showband era was 'The Hucklebuck' by Brendan Bowyer. In fact it was the

B-side to 'I Ran All The Way Home'. When recording it, they played it once, as they did it on stage, and then got Brendan to over-dub the lead vocal while the lads clapped along and shouted 'Hey!' at the breaks.

Eamon Andrews Studios and the TV Club

Most of the early band recordings were done at the Eamon Andrews Studios based in Henry Street and later at the TV Club on Harcourt Street in Dublin. The facilities at the time were very basic with most recordings being done on a four track recording machine, the highest standard of equipment available at the time! Even a lot of the early Beatles stuff was on four track. All the backing was put down on three tracks while the fourth was kept for the vocals. The Beatles recorded mainly in the Abbey Road Studios where The Royal Showband also recorded 'The Hucklebuck' in November 1964.

A lot of the big hits of the mid 1960s were recorded in Henry Street. Most of Joe Dolan's earlier hits were done there but I believe his first recording, 'The Answer to Everything', was recorded in Bray where The Drifters just set up the gear as if on stage and played and sang in similar fashion.

Speaking of Joe, one of his biggest hits, 'The Whitewashed Gable', was a cover of an American hit called '246 West Maple' but his management reckoned the title was a little bit too American for the Irish market so the house got a 'whitewash' makeover. Brilliant! A lot of the bands recorded slow sentimental songs about orphans, drunken drivers and broken hearts, preferably in an old time waltz tempo.

Towards the end of the Sixties, John Dardis opened Trend

Studios in Lad Lane where he offered very good rates and attracted some of the less affluent musicians from middle-of-the-road bands and beat groups. At one time, he had a special deal going where you could record an LP (three days studio time) for £100.

A lot of beat groups used Trend Studios for demo tape sessions when trying to break into the big time. I well remember one compilation album that Trend produced called, 'Paddy Is Dead and the Kids Know It'! What a great title, and the album featured a lot of the Dublin groups of the time like Skid Row and Chosen Few. The title was suggesting the paddywackery days of the showband were over with the onslaught of the beat group. I'm not so sure if the sentiment was correct, but it was an adventurous album with a clever title featuring some good groups of the time.

Session Men

When it came to recording, not many bands actually played the backing music on their own records. While most showband musicians were very good live performers, they sometimes found it difficult to perform well in a studio environment. This is quite common across the board in the music industry, in classical, country and even jazz. Playing in a studio is a much different discipline to playing live and each individual has their own comfort zone. People who are not used to studio work tend to get nervous and start making simple mistakes with the result that something that should only take three hours might end up taking a lot longer. So, as studio time can be expensive, it made a lot of sense just to let the professionals at it. The other side of the coin was that sometimes the recordings were too plush and lacked that raw, fresh, loose feeling of the live performance. Also, there was the problem of finding time to record, with lots of bands playing five and six nights a week. This only left Mondays for recordings and, as most of the studios were in Dublin or Belfast, this presented a problem for the rural bands. Another factor, of course, was that some of the guys were simply not good enough to play on the recordings. It was always a big secret, with everyone pretending that we all played on everything.

Some musicans used to get uptight about the use of session men on some of their band's recordings. What would people think if they heard we weren't playing on our records? Well it happened elsewhere too. In the UK, there was a big hullabaloo in the press when British group Love Affair were accused of not playing their instruments on their hit single 'Everlasting Love'. Similiarly, it was reported that the American group The Byrds did not play on 'Mr Tambourine Man'.

So what, sure Elvis or Cliff didn't play guitar or drums on their records either. Even Ringo didn't play on some early Beatle singles. And what about the group of session men in the States who recorded a song called 'Lets Go To San Francisco' and released it under the name of The Flowerpot Men. Of course, it made the charts and they then had the headache of recruiting musicians to tour under that name. A group of British session men had a similar experience when they released 'I was Kaiser Bill's Batman' under the name of Whistling Jack Smith.

So, here you had these bored session heads recording these things for the craic and having international hits by default, while the rest of us were standing on our heads trying to think of some way we could stroke our way into the local charts. And then we had to listen to some fellas worrying about what they'd do if the local postman found out that they didn't actually play on the latest 'masterpiece' they had just inflicted on an unsuspecting public. God give us patience!

With the introduction of the Irish Top Ten in the early Sixties, some of the top bands started to record and so gradually everybody felt compelled to make records in the hope of making the charts. The trend up to then for publicity was that you would buy a page in the national or provincial press and get promoters and businesses to congratulate you when you got new suits, or were five years on the road, or doing your first American tour; any excuse to get the coverage. As I said, the band would buy the page and get people to support them. If you were from a provincial town you would approach the local businesses and local ballrooms and most of them would support you. There would be a big spoof written about the band for whatever the occasion was, a new girl singer or maybe a new record.

When a band released a record, publicity became easier because each play on the radio, Radio Éireann as it was then, was as good as ten pages in the national or local papers. As most bands worked a particular region, they may not have been doing as well elsewhere. But when you got radio play it helped when ringing a guy in Donegal or Wexford and you could say, 'Did you hear our record? It got three or four plays during the week.'

It was a great door-opener. However, it led to all sorts of abuses with every tin whistle band wanting to record and if they weren't great musically they would be in trouble. They'd have session people for the recording which would make them sound like a symphony orchestra and the fact that they couldn't reproduce the sound on stage didn't seem to really bother them. They figured on getting the punters in first and then worrying about the sound.

There were abuses in it just like everything else, such as buying records into the charts, but it was all part of it. There was nothing unique in this, it also went on in the UK. In our day you also had to get some plugger to get you on the play list because, without that, you just wouldn't get played.

So how would you get on the play list? It's the old 'chicken or egg' situation. The talk I hear these days about boybands and girlbands going straight in at number one, well it just makes me laugh, it's unbelievable! To me, it's like forming a new football team and winning the Premiership in your first season. There's been a lot of talk of money coming into the business through the financial rise of the 'tweenie', eight-to twelve-year-olds buying CDs and downloading music. But I don't care what hype there is, somebody is helping somebody along the way. In an early interview, Louis Walsh said he learned all the tricks of the trade during the showband days when he worked in Tommy Hayden's office. Tommy managed people like Linda Martin and Johnny Logan and all sorts of famous artists from Eurovision land.

Sponsored Programmes

Again going back to the Sixties, there were sponsored programmes such as Andrews Liver Salts, Imco, Prescotts Cleaners and others. These programmes were 15 minute slots presented by DJs like Larry Gogan, Val Joyce, Brendan Balfe and Gay Byrne. These poor guys were haunted by every showband manager in the land trying to promote their latest and greatest biggest star in the land. The guys couldn't enjoy their sambo and soup in Madigans in Moore Street without some 'silver tongued impressario' appearing with a bundle of vinyl singles tucked under his arm. This latest masterpiece was the greatest thing since sliced pan and luckily he had one for everybody within an ass's roar of the place. And if he ran short, sure he had plenty more in the boot of the car as he was buying them by the box in every record shop he could find. Folks, this story is true, I should know, because unfortunately I have to admit that I was one of these 'gombeen' managers! Poor Larry Gogan and the lads were plagued with us trying to get them to play our records but sometimes they didn't have the picking of the music. It was the producers or the advertising agencies that selected the music so you would have to try and get in the backdoor to those people too.

I remember there was a show on Friday afternoons around 1.15pm, hosted by Gay Byrne when he would play some of the new releases. He would give his comments on what he thought and I remember on one show there was a new singer being launched. He was quite a nice singer in the Jim Reeves mould but, like a lot of guys, he had a little problem with timing and tuning, so Gay's comment went something like this, 'I don't mind you practicing how to sing, young man, but not on my show, thank you very much.'

Hyping . . . With A Little Help From Your Friends!

As regards recordings and making records, the big thing was the airplay. The market share was so small that it didn't matter what you sold. For one of our 'hits', The Millionaires received a royalty cheque for the massive sum of 19 shillings and 6 pence, not even £1. No wonder we were The Millionaires! But it didn't matter what you sold or what you didn't sell, it was all about the amount of airplay you got, that was the key thing.

However, bands would go to any lengths to get a hit record. We had a situation where we used to tour America a lot and we always watched out for whatever was in the American charts to see if it would also suit the Irish market. We had a contact there who used to send us over the records, whatever he thought would be suitable. One time he sent us over two lovely records but didn't put enough stamps on the parcel so by the time we got them, they had already been covered and released in Ireland. One was 'The Unicorn' and the other was 'Simon Says' by the Bubblegum Company. Dickie Rock released 'Simon Says' while The Irish Rovers covered 'The Unicorn'.

If only we had got them in time, we would have been huge stars. Another case of 'we woz robbed, guv'. Also, when a band would release a record, they would hype it up by buying them themselves in an effort to get them into the Top 20. You might get in at number 19 or get up to 15, and you would then buy and buy trying to help it climb the charts. Sometimes, if the people actually liked it then it would genuinely move up the charts, but in most cases it was hyped in and as soon as you stopped buying, it would go straight back out.

There was a great story about a well known west of Ireland band that had a very good record. They bought a few just to get it started and it entered at number nine. They then decided to buy some more to push it up and when they listened to the Top 10 the next week, number nine, number seven, number five, no sign of it.

'Ah, it must have gone out again, well feck it anyway, we should have bought more.'

But hadn't it got to number two! The plan was they would buy a little more each week and this would gradually push it up the charts but they didn't allow for the fact that a lot of people actually liked the record and went out and bought it so it was a genuine hit. It caught them off guard when it went straight from nine to two and then to number one in just three weeks, what a waste! The ideal plan would be to get it in at a low position and move slowly, taking as long as possible to move up say two or three places at a time which would mean that you could be in the Top 20 for anything up to ten weeks. Going straight from nine to two, while it was great in one sense, it only gave you a lifespan of five to six weeks at most.

Posters and Promotions

During my tenure as manager of The Raindrops we recorded two singles for release on the Irish market in the early Seventies. The first one featured Chris Grace on lead vocals with 'Less of Me' and 'Lonely Town'. Chris was no stranger to the recording business having tasted Top 10 successes with The Donie Collins' Band during the mid-Sixties with a lovely version of the old Tab Hunter song, 'Young Love'. We really went to town on the promotion of that record and our poster campaign took us from Donegal to Kerry. Our plan of action was never to leave Galway without a bundle of posters and a bucket of paste, so that on the return journey after the gig, during the early hours of the morning, we could be found bill posting under the moonlight. It didn't matter what part of the country we were in, we'd spend an hour or two plastering every vantage point along the way, on the back of road signs, ESB poles and bridges. Nowhere was safe when we got going!

One night while we were in full flight, Ollie Maloney and his band arrived on the scene and pulled up to have a slag with us. So, while I was chatting away with Ollie and the boys, some of our lads sneaked around his van and plastered it with The Raindrops posters. By the time they'd have arrived back home in Tuam I'm sure the paste was well dry on the van. I'd say our ears were red with the boys praying for us as they tried to remove our offending posters from their minibus!

We got quite a lot of plays for 'Less of Me' as it was our first record, but it was a nice song with a nice peace theme, 'Be a little kinder; think a little more of others and a little less of me.'

Our next single was a double A side, featuring Dermot Walsh singing, 'Knock On My Window' and Brendan Mulhaire on accordion with a funky version of 'The Mason's Apron'. Strangely enough, it was the instrumental side that caught the attention of the DJs and captured most of the plays, possibly because it was very different and quite adventurous for that time.

This was one of the occasions where we used session men on the recordings with both Des Moore (session guitarist and brother of Butch Moore) and drummer Johnny Wadham producing some very funky sounds. I remember talking to Wadham later about that recording and he told me he actually bought the record to see how it sounded as he quite enjoyed playing on it.

'I don't buy too many showband records, you know,' he remarked with a wry smile. Somehow, I believed him!

The making of a record was a pretty expensive exercise, especially for bands in the lower divisions. So why did they make them? For the publicity of course. Getting your band's record played on national radio meant that you had immediate access to the ears of every promoter and hall owner in the country. While a lot of these guys might not take your calls it was one way of getting through to them. Of course, you would have to follow up with all sorts of spoof with mail shots and media promotions to the provincial press, telling them what a great hit this record was. It really didn't matter whether the record sold or not, what was most important was getting airplay. It was a bonus if it did sell enough to make the charts because it gave you a bit more to negotiate with.

Radio Éireann, Ruth & Co

Now that The Raindrops had made this amazing new recording on the Ruby record label, I headed for Dublin, the Mecca of the entertainment business, with nothing on my mind but to make this masterpiece the hit it deserved to be! Having dropped off the famous press releases at the *Evening Press*, *Evening Herald* and *Spotlight* for the various journalists, I then headed for Radio Éireann on Henry Street. With my little box of records under my arm I got on the lift that would take me to the top floor where the radio studios were housed. Just before the lift took off I was joined by a lady whom I immediately recognised as being the lovely Ruth Buchanan.

As we headed skywards, I naturally enough was telling my captive audience, poor Ruth, about my mission and politely asked her if she knew where I could find any of the lads, you know, the disc jockeys, Larry and the boys! Ruth very kindly said she'd show me where the reception was and that I could leave the records there with security who would put one into each pigeon hole for the various presenters and she was sure they would all get them. Brilliant!

With that the lift stopped, 'ping' went the bell and the door opened. Well, I couldn't believe my eyes, I thought I must be in heaven, because who did I see standing right in front of me only the three wise men: Larry Gogan, Mike Murphy and Noel Andrews. Everybody was smiling and nodding to each other. Ruth and myself got out and Larry and the boys got in. Before the lads could press the button I did a quick U-turn, thinking to myself, sure aren't these the very lads I'm looking for. So, as Ruth walked away out of my life forever, I jumped straight back into the lift with the lads!

We all got out at the ground floor, and as I hadn't fully finished telling them all about this great new release I had for them, we headed on down Henry Street, turned right and upstairs into the lounge of Madigans on Moore Street. While we were having our soup and sambos, I presented each of them with their own 'personal' copy of The Raindrops' latest release.

The lads seemed to be very interested as I was giving them the background as to how the record was made. During the course of our time in Madigans we were joined occasionally by some of their colleagues and I made sure that nobody was left out, they all received a single. Even Brendan Balfe, whom I approached by saying, 'I'm sure by now you must have at least two thousand showband records.'

To which he graciously replied, 'You're right, but it has always been my ambition to have two thousand and one, so thank you very much!'

I'm very pleased to report that every one of those guys gave our records a few spins and on behalf of all the gombeen band managers of Ireland, I'd like to say a big thank you to them all, because you may not realise it, but it helped a lot at the time. You see, some of these masterpieces were never actually released, a lot of them simply 'escaped' and some of them should have been put down! So you can take a bow and share in some of the blame and shame by your actions.

And as for that Ruth Buchanan one, she never once called, wrote or phoned, so I'm not going to bother either!

Sponsored Programmes

Then there was *Spotlight* magazine which was the bible of the Irish entertainment business at the time. In those days the British ones were *Melody Maker* and *New Musical Express* which people might know as the *NME*. In the States there was *Rolling Stone*. To get a write-up in *Spotlight* you had to buy a lot of advertising but you would get reporters here and there who would do daft profiles on bands asking questions about their new single, favourite food, car, sport, pastime and the age of the band members. With regard to the latter, funny enough it was always between 18 and 28. There were very few in the band business over the age of 25, definitely no older than 28. It didn't matter how you looked, grey hair and all, you were never over 28.

Some of the publicity ideas were ridiculous but new bands had to try very hard. For instance, *Spotlight* ran a theme feature where one week they had Tony and the Graduates going around a university as graduate students. The next week they had The

Casino in a casino gambling away and The Cadets on a ship. Then The Millionaires were brought down Grafton Street, where we staged a mock bank robbery. Three of us entered the bank with fake guns and then ran out the door where the other members of the band were waiting with the 'getaway car', a Guinness horse-drawn dray which we had borrowed for the afternoon. We had all the people on the street and in buses looking on at the spectacle. We would not have attempted this a couple of years later after the 'Troubles' started, but the mid Sixties were more innocent times.

Managers and Agents – Spoofers and Chancers

As the business got more successful, it attracted every sort of gombeen man and get-rich-quick type. There were a lot of gallery merchants, stroke merchants, spoofers, sharks and vultures. Everyone wanted to be connected to a band, to get a piece of the action. It's like the football scene in the UK, hanging on to whoever is the personality of the week, but the old showband scene seemed to attract an extra few. It was amazing how many business people wanted to buy into the business. It attracted every sort of an eejit, as if we didn't have enough of our own home-grown material. Then there were the spoofers, hype merchants and record pushers.

Agencies, Lead Singers and *Spotlight*

When the agencies started to expand, you'd have a situation whereby the agent with one good band could launch another one on the strength of the main band. In general, the new band would be good but it was like selling Guinness products. When they launch a new beer they make the publicans take a certain amount of the new product in order to get the main branded product that they really wanted. I am thinking of the time that The Miami was launched. They were in the same stable as The Capitol. Every promoter or hall owner wanted The Capitol but if you got a Capitol date then you had to take a booking for one of the smaller bands. A lot of the new bands were good and The Miami were excellent and could stand on their own feet, but there were some gluggers along the way which were pushed in. This made it very hard for the smaller, single-agent bands. Another development was that people were looking for a front man like Dickie Rock with The Miami. It attracted English has-beens, guys who had been big in England and faded into the background. I am thinking of guys like Houston Wells who came and joined The Premier Aces. He was a country singer and suited them very well. Rickie Valance came and joined The Chessmen. The problem was managers would make up all sorts of rubbish and put it into the newspapers and this is still going on to this very day. Fine if you knew and understood what was happening but some of the guys started to believe what they read about themselves in *Spotlight* and that's when the trouble started. 'But I am the third best singer in Ireland and I have the biggest listenership. It says it here in *Spotlight*.'

The publicity machine would be the local press. It would be up to the ballrooms to try and get features for visiting bands whose managers were never shy about writing to the local and national papers prompting them to carry features on their 'latest and greatest talents'. For the *Evening Press*, Billy Duffy compiled the 'Paul Jones Diary' while for the *Evening Herald*, Michael Ryan and Tony Wilson succeeded Frank Hall in writing the 'Tempo Pages'. There were features, photographs and write-ups which were all part of the publicity machine, nowadays called marketing. If a band had a manager this was part of his job, but if there was no manager, the band leader would organise coverage and try to tie it in to the touring or the promoting of a new record. It was all part of the machine. Then you had *Spotlight* magazine where, if you bought an advert, you got a bit of editorial.

Every year you had 'Ireland's Top Ten Bands'. One year there was actually 11 bands as there was a dead heat for tenth place!

Managers – Picking the Team

A lot of the fun went out of the scene when managers got involved. It became big business then, cut-throat business. There were guys coming in who didn't have a clue about music but saw an opportunity, got in there and manufactured bands to play conveyer-belt music.

There was a case where a band had eight members and the manager wanted to bring in a girl singer. He looked at the band and said, 'There's a singer there who doesn't play an instrument, and a bass player who doesn't sing.' They couldn't have two singers standing there 'doing nothing' so he decided the bass player had to go.

Someone asked, 'What are we doing to do for a bass player'?

He said 'Well I see the trumpet player and the singer playing a bit of bass, so ye can play it between ye.'

Now, the 'bit of bass' would be simple stuff played during the interval, when three would go for a tea-break and three would play. You only needed to learn three tunes on the bass, dum,

dum, dum, dum to cover this easy stuff, and the trombone player might sit behind the drums.

But the manager, who didn't know anything about music and obviously saw things rather than heard them, said, 'Didn't I see you playing it?'

In the heel of the hunt anyway, the bass player had to go to make way for the girl, the male singer had to learn how to play another little bit of bass and the trumpet player did another little bit on bass also. Eventually, the singer turned out to be a reasonable bass player. But that was the way it was, the new era after the managers came in. So it all changed, it became more ruthless. The manager, with his contacts with other managers and venue promoters, took the power then and the musicians became secondary. Often you were at their mercy but, to be fair, some managers did a lot of good for the business also.

Wages or Co-op Bands

Earlier I talked a bit about the regional bands and the different categories. I think 1958 was about the time The Clipper Carlton, The Melody Aces and The Johnny Flynn Band started to make an impact on the dancing scene. Johnny would have been known as John Joe and later JJ Flynn but as time passed, 'Johnny' became trendier. I suppose another in that category would be Donie Collins. He owned the band, he would hire the musicians and pay them by the night and eventually he paid them by the week. I suppose Donie Collins and Johnny Flynn would be similar in this regard because they would have four or five nights a week so they could guarantee musicians so much a week. I think eventually they went on wages which involved a flat wage for say four nights and if you did an extra night there would be a bonus for the fifth or sixth night. That generally was how they operated but I am sure there were some exceptions to the rule.

Take Donie Collins for instance. He owned the band, he ran the band, paid all the bills and he managed the band as well. He was one of these lads who liked to keep things close to his chest. Others, like Johnny Flynn, appointed a manager, Miko Kelly. Miko worked in the post office in Tuam and his counterpart with The Clippers also worked in the post office in Strabane. They didn't travel with the band; they did the bookings and the administration work because at that time both bands were in huge demand. Another band like that was The Premier Aces from Roscommon, who used to publish their Dancing Diary with the List of Dates for the week every Saturday in the *Irish Independent*. From that alone they were consistently working so they had to be presenting a popular show.

We hear a lot of talk about the fortunes made by people involved in the showband industry during the Sixties. Well, I can tell that this was not the case for the vast majority of musicians. While there's no denying that some people did make big money over the years, if you look at the bigger picture it tells a different story.

If we take the period from 1960 to 1965, I believe that the promoters made all the money as most bands were on a straight fee. Then, from about 1965 onwards, some of the bigger, more popular bands could command a percentage of the door takings and were receiving between 50 and 60 per cent. But remember, this applied only to the top 20 or maybe 50 bands. Therefore, the remaining 500 or so bands in the lower brackets were paid straight fees according to their rating in the pecking order.

Also, it was around this time that some bands starting working on a co-op basis which meant that the musicians were receiving a share of the takings as distinct from a straight wage, resulting in the boys getting a more even share of the spoils.

Here are some examples from my experience.

In 1961, I was playing two or three nights a week and being paid 30 shillings per night, while at the same time I was paid 30 shillings for a six day week serving my time in a drapery shop. The average weekly factory wage was around £5 while Johnny Flynn was paying up to £25 per week.

By 1970, fees for mid-range bands like The Raindrops were roughly £100–150 on Sundays; £60–80 on Fridays; and £40–60 midweek. A weekly average for the full band was in the region of £200–250, while some big bands would get this for one night.

Musicians and artistic people in general are not known for their good financial management skills.

Managers, Agencies, Fees and Percentages

Fees and percentages would have started in the mid Sixties. The bands were on a bigger fee and some of them started to command a percentage. The first band of the percentage era was The Royal; they were so popular that they could command pretty much what they wanted. They were the leaders and TJ Byrne was the man there, Ireland's answer to Colonel Parker. He was the complete manager. He did everything from bookings to marketing, mentoring and even advice on sound. But he managed just one band, The Royal Showband, so it was a professional enough operation. It was when the guys started getting the agencies going, that's where it started to get a little bit hairy.

There were a lot of decent people involved but there were also many wheeler-dealers who got into it. The problem was with the guys that 'jumped on the bandwagon'. (Sorry about the pun but what an apt expression.) Managers, a lot of them would just get the dates, put an oul' ad in *Spotlight* and get a bit of publicity going, while some other managers did everything really. Generally, it was getting the dates and hyping up the band. The more hype they generated, the easier it was to get the dates. Band managers were basically salesmen. They just lived on the phone, spoofing, hustling and hassling, and if they had a good band it helped.

Remember that bands made their living by playing at gigs and they had to work four or five nights a week to survive. The manager's job was to get you as high up the scale as possible by getting into the bigger halls and venues. Some of the bands were genuinely good crowd pullers with good shows, but a lot of the bands in latter years were just hyped up by their managers. They would get a short run at it with any sort of gimmick and they would keep changing tack. If things were beginning to wane they would change the singer or put out a new record. It didn't matter if it sold or not, they would get it played and if you were a manager who had a name or a knack for getting things played on RTÉ, then you were really ahead of the posse.

So, that's what it came down to in the end. The manager with the right contacts and the greatest amount of hassle could muscle in and just keep ahead. The more they got into that end of things, the harder it was for the lads with an ordinary band

and an ordinary manager who were going on merit alone. Unfortunately, performing on merit became the hardest job of all.

From the 1970s onwards, things took a turn towards country and Irish music when the likes of Release Records started promoting that end of things. They had a good professional operation and they worked hard at getting the radio plays so they wound up dictating the policy to a degree. I know patrons liked that sound as well, but it was a move away from the original showband scene. Things became confusing with some bands going country and others moving towards the pop scene. I suppose what really happened was that two markets emerged, a pop market and a country one, but there was always a bigger market for the country and Irish stuff. Me? Well, I always preferred the original showband music!

The Eurovision
Getting a record played on radio or an appearance on television was a great boost for any band but the biggest break a band could get was to have your singer picked to represent Ireland in the Eurovision Song Contest. Every year around February, RTÉ would hold a national competition to select an act to go forward to the European finals. The first stage was to select about 12 songs from the hundreds of songs entered for the national competition and the next part was to pick singers to perform each song.

For a singer or an act to be invited to take part in the national contest was indeed a great honour, so needless to say there was always great competition and debate as to who might get the call.

After all, a spot on primetime TV was always good for publicity no matter how good or bad the song might be. As the saying goes, there is no such thing as bad publicity! As well as all the publicity there was a cash prize for the composer of the winning song ,with a bonus of an extra few quid if the winning song was in Irish. This bonus prize was only ever won once, when Sandie Jones sang 'Ceol an Ghrá'! Sonny Knowles was a regular competitor in the national contest, and although he never succeeded in singing the winning song, he was still involved on most of the final nights, playing saxophone in the orchestra. Sonny always got the gig.

There was no doubt about it, but if having a hit record meant a boost for business, then representing Ireland in the Eurovision Song Contest was like winning the Lotto for any singer or band in the early days of the competition. While Butch Moore and Dickie Rock already were big names before their Eurovision success, it did raise their popularity to another level. However, for the likes of Sean Dunphy, Pat McGeegan, Muriel Day, Tina, Red Hurley and the Swarbriggs, it did wonders for their respective bands. They attracted much bigger crowds to their dance dates and after all, that was where the bands made their money, in the ballrooms and marquees throughout the country, not from record sales.

For many years it appeared that the powers that be in the Dublin agencies, seemed to have a franchise on the Eurovision thing. At one stage, when Joe Dolan was asked what he thought of the Eurovision, he quipped, 'I wouldn't know anything about it, sure I'm not from Dublin!'

Nine

Born for the USA

Off to the States

It's an ill-wind, they say, that doesn't blow some good. In other words, what is one person's misfortune could be someone else's good fortune. This turned out to be the case for my buddies and myself in The International Showband with the break-up of The Clipper Carlton. It's well accepted in the business, and most people would agree, that The Clippers were the guys that started it all. They were the first showband.

Both individually and collectively, they were all well respected musicians and added to this was their great ability to entertain. They put on a cabaret show they called 'Juke Box Saturday Night' which included comedy and impersonations.

Unfortunately, there comes a time sooner or later when good things come to an end and this turned out to be the case with their break-up in the autumn of 1964. They had one final row and they split. Obviously, this was to cause big problems for some

185

promoters, including Bill Fuller who had booked them for a three-week tour of the main Irish centres in New York, Boston and Chicago. When the search started for a replacement band for the US tour, our name was quickly thrown into the hat by our manager who, as luck would have it, was also managing the Astoria in Manchester for the aforementioned Mr Bill Fuller. So, with a little gentle pressure being provided by our management, the bould Bill was persuaded to take the 'Fantastic International Showband' (from Galway) on their first trip to the good old US in October 1964.

Landing on the Moon

There's no doubt about it, but when I arrived in the US it was like landing on the moon. Television had only reached Ireland on a national scale a few years earlier, around 1962, and up to that all we had seen about America would have been through the movies. So, landing in the middle of it was like a dream really.

I have often described it as like falling asleep in your local cinema while watching a film and waking up to find that you were actually in the movie, yellow cabs, the lot. I'd say I was back home a few weeks after my first visit before it sank in that I had really been there, and I couldn't wait to go again.

Before we left, however, we had the usual panic over visas but, as always, we banked on them being sorted out by the time we would be going home!

Boston was our first stop and with our Galway connections we couldn't have started in a better place, we just couldn't go wrong! On the night we arrived we were only in the hotel room about half an hour when the phone rang.

'What kept ye? I've been ringing all day looking for ye,' said this female voice. It's Gay Meehan, our old friend from home. She and her boyfriend arrive at the hotel to take us out to eat, our first taste of the great American menu. As they ordered, all I could hear was: iced water, paper napkins, open turkey sandwich, coleslaw, American pie. Christ, it was like a Christmas dinner!

We were staying in this massive hotel, the Sherry Biltmore, and Freddie Teite, the Belfast boxer, was there as well on his own. The elevator didn't stop at the thirteenth floor. You got static electric shocks from the door handles and the central heating blew only dry air. You might say we were only getting used to mod-cons!

Our very first night was in Watertown, a small venue on the outskirts of Boston. For logistical reasons, it didn't make sense for us to drag our equipment all the way across the Atlantic so, with the exception of our own individual instruments, everything else was hired. When we arrived at the venue all the gear was there with a PA system and a control console plonked right in the middle of the small stage. Of course, being America, everything else was big, including the sound man behind the controls.

Picture the scene in Watertown, Massachusetts. Opening gig of our very first tour of the US of A. Sinatra country, a big PA system, a console plus operator, the whole bit, the real deal. Showtime approaches and it's time for a sound check.

'Testing, one two three. Nothing is happening, what's wrong?'

'It just don't work like it did today, what can I do?' Yeah, that's what the man said. But in the meantime we had a gig to do and all we had was a dead PA system and a half-alive driver and they taking up half the stage. Go to plan B, Operation Panic!

Luckily for us, the promoter had arranged for Des Regan and George Shanley, a traditional Irish group, to play as a support opening spot. Enter good old Dessie. 'I've got my wedding PA kit in the trunk of the car,' says he.

'So what are we waiting for?' says I. 'Get it in here.'

And within twenty minutes, Dessie has all his gear set up. With two 12" monitor speakers out front and a redundant console and driver at the back, we were all set to go with the best PA system in Watertown that night. Eat your heart out Old Blue Eyes. Welcome to America, musically speaking!

We found out very quickly that our American audience weren't really interested in the 'Great American Songbook' and couldn't care less about what was in the British charts. What they wanted to hear was music that reminded them of home, songs that would take them back to the local halls they had left behind in Ireland. Our saviour was to be 'the musical tour of Ireland' which was a medley of Irish waltzes we had learned especially for the tour. The idea being that each guy in the band, in turn, would sing a song from a different county in Ireland, from Cork to Dublin and from Derry to Kerry. This medley and I were to become great friends, being passed from band to band over the years and even today we still do it at weddings.

Next stop, the New State Ballroom in Boston of Glenn Miller fame, the first of the Bill Fuller chain of ballrooms. The good thing about the bigger venues was the fact that they had resident bands and we could use their equipment which was usually top of the range.

As I have already mentioned, musicians loved touring because it was akin to going on holiday abroad. You got the

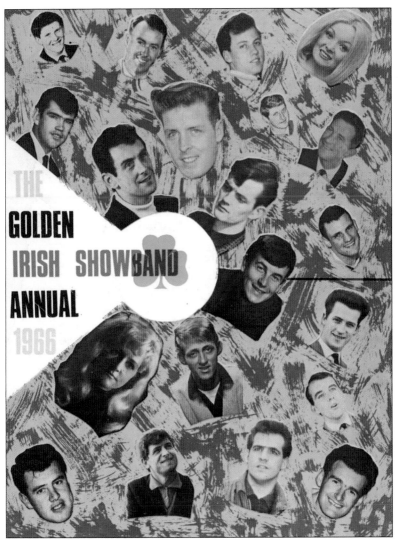

This is the front cover of the Golden Irish Showband Annual 1966. The stars featured here include (from the top) Tony Keeling, Dermot O'Brien, Kelley, Derek Dean, Pat McGeegan, Roy Donn, Larry Cunningham, Brian Coll, Butch Moore, Sean Fagan, Eileen Reid, Dickie Rock, Tommy Drennan, Brendan Bowyer, DJ Curtin, Joe Dolan, Tom Dunphy.

COUNTRY FOLK

When Margo decided to go solo, her backing band, the Country Folk, played on featuring two singers, Frankie Carroll and Frankie McCaffrey. Looking more like 'Country Gents' than 'Country Folk' they set about cleaning up their act! They obviously hadn't made it to their hairdresser when this photo was taken! (L to R) Paddy Higgins, Michael Keane, Frank McCaffrey, Jim Malone, Transport Manager (?!), Dave Trainer, Kieran Murphy, Frankie Carroll.

The New York Showband featuring Tommy Flynn (ex Conquerors). (L to R) John Meehan from Queens, on accordion, Ron Eisenberg from Brooklyn on bass guitar, Tommy Flynn from County Clare – vocalist, Paddy Higgins from County Galway on drums, Michael O'Driscoll from County Kilkenny on guitar and bass synthesiser. With the demise of the Country Folk, my brother Paddy got a haircut and moved to New York where he played for many years with Christy O'Connor and Sean Fleming before moving to Las Vegas to play with Brendan Bowyer.

The Billy Brown Band – Musically speaking, this was probably one of the best line-ups ever seen in this country! However, as in music or sport, you know what they say about a group of stars not always being the most successful outfit. Whether it was due to the fact that they played above the people's heads or that unfortunately Billy was experiencing some bad health at the time, this great band had a very short run. Line-up left to right Johnny Browne (bass), Mick Nolan (trumpet), Dessie Reynolds (drums), Tiger Taylor (guitar), Billy Brown (keys/sax/vocals), Pat Haverty (sax), Keith Donald (sax).

Shaun O'Dowd – Ding-A-Ling

Tweed

As we moved through the Seventies there was a very definite division in styles. While the country music scene was very strong, there was also plenty of scope for the pop/rock market. There were many fine bands doing good business, for example: The Plattermen, Freshmen, Memories, Chips, Gentry, Real McCoy, Times, Sands, Philosophers, Tweed and Shaun O'Dowd and Ding-A-Ling. On one side of the coin we had country singers with dancing fiddlers, banjos and Hawaiian steel guitars, while on the flip-side we had rockers with coloured shirts and curly heads, 'getting on down' with 'Glam Rock Glitter'.

The Big 8

For over 20 years the unity of the Royal was rock solid, so it was no wonder that the showband world was shocked by the news of a split in the ranks. Tom Dunphy and Brendan Bowyer were leaving to form a superband to be managed by former colleague T. J. Byrne. Every musician in the country was waiting for the call and when the chosen few were announced it included the who's who of showbandland. Led by the great Paddy Cole, the star studded line-up featured Twink, Dave Coady, Mickey O'Neill, Jimmy Conway and Michael Keane. They became so popular in Las Vegas that they eventually moved there permanently. Due to the untimely death of Tom Dunphy, Galwayman Frankie Carroll took over on bass/vocals. Others who worked with the Big 8 over the years included Kelley, Helen Jordan, Lola (vocals), Paddy Reynolds, Pat Chesters, D.J. Curtin (saxophone), Tommy Burke (trumpet) and Paddy Higgins (drums).

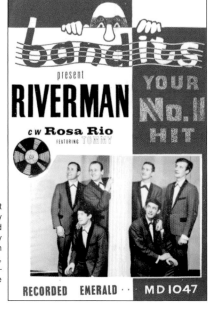

This is a poster of the Bandits promoting their first record Riverman/Rosa Rio. Managed by Ray O'Brien of Western Promotions, this Tuam-based band had their own show on Radio Éireann every Monday night. The record featured Tommy Ryan on vocals/bass guitar, Eamon Ryan – lead guitar, Jimmy Reilly – saxophone, Willie Brogan – trombone, Stan McCormack – trumpet and Donie Trout on drums.

This photo of the Raindrops with Padraic O'Conaire was taken in Eyre Square, Galway in 1969. It was used as part of the promotional material for their American tour in March of that year. The Irish Americans loved the hand-outs as souvenirs of Galway. The Raindrops line-up at that time was (from the front) Brendan Mulhaire, Jimmy Higgins, John Conneely, (back) Eamon Joyce, Billy Barrett, Chris Grace, Dermot Walsh.

'Hairy' Raindrops
You've hair today and hopefully you'll have more tomorrow! As we moved into the Seventies, the hair got longer and the clothes more colourful! There were a few changes in personnel and the line-up now was Jimmy Higgins, Vinnie Mongan, Brendan Mulhaire, Eamon Joyce, Francie Higgins, Billy Barrett.

The Big Time
How to get into the Big Time? Get a new drummer like Walty Lynch, two young singers like Johnny Sheilds and Dessie O'Neill and put them out front. Then all you need is some yellow shirts, shiny jackets and car stickers inviting you to 'Follow the Big Time' and you're on your way! Well, that was the plan anyway.

MOYLOUGH

CARNIVAL

APRIL 30th - MAY 14th, 1961

Dancing in Spacious Marquee with Maple Floor
CARNIVAL NOVELTIES AND VALUABLE SPOT PRIZES

— PROGRAMME —

SUNDAY, April 30th: Adm., 6/-.

DENIS CRONIN
AND HIS ORCHESTRA, TRALEE

TUESDAY, May 2nd: Adm., 6/-.

Maurice Mulcahy
AND HIS 15-PIECE ORCHESTRA.

THURSDAY, May 4th: Adm., 5/-.

DES FRETWELL
AND HIS ORCHESTRA, GALWAY.

FRI., May 5:   Ceili & Fancy Dress   Adm., 4/-.

JACKIE HEARST
CEILI BAND.

SUNDAY, May 7th: Adm., 6/-.

JACK BARRETT
AND HIS DANCE ORCHESTRA.

TUESDAY, May 9th: Adm., 5/-.

DONIE COLLINS
AND HIS ORCHESTRA, ASKEATON.

THURSDAY, May 11th: Adm., 6/-.

JIMMY WILEY
DANCE ORCHESTRA (Mitchelstown)

FRIDAY, May 12th.   Adm., 5/-

PREMIER ACES
SHOW BAND

SUNDAY, May 14th.   Adm., 6/-.

DAVE DIXON
CLONES.

Sunday, April 30th: Children's Fancy Dress at 3 p.m.

Sunday, May 7th: Children's 7-a-Side School Football.
Thursday, May 11th: 7-a-Side Football Matches.

Sunday, May 14th: Children's Sports.

NOTE: RAS GAILLIMHE, April 23rd.   100 Miles Cycle Race. Starting from Moylough at 2 p.m.

Song 9-3.   ★   Season Tickets, 35/- from W. Fallon.   ★   Catering by Ladies Committee.   ★   Mineral Bar.

This poster for Moylough Carnival for May 1961 was the standard type of poster printed by the *Tuam Herald* for festivals/carnivals around that time. All the details were covered. Dancing in spacious marquee, carnival novelties and spot prizes, football 7-a-side, children's fancy dress and sports day, catering by ladies' committee. It would run for two weeks with dancing on Sundays, Tuesdays, Thursdays and Fridays. The style of the bands at that time was mixed – there were dance orchestras and céilí bands. The Premier Aces were the only showband on the bill. Notice all the bands were called after their leader – i.e. Maurice Mulcahy, Donie Collins, Dave Dixon – as the showband was just coming into fashion around that time.

The marquee in this photo is typical of the standard used for dancing in Ireland during the Sixties. The size varied from a 4-pole, 5-pole or 6-pole depending on the popularity of the location. Usually the small stage was mounted on cement blocks with a mineral bar and ladies' cloakroom on either side. Power was sourced from the nearest house by the local electrician and the band speakers were hung on the first pole if your lead was long enough. Despite these most basic of facilities, there was a great atmosphere in marquee dancing even on a wet night.

This brochure only shows part of the programme of events for the Dungloe carnival. As you can see they have dancing on Sunday, Tuesday, Thursday and Friday of each week, with a céilí on Wednesday. All top acts including Big Tom, Margo, Brian Coll and Buckaroos [with Arty McGlynn] and Eurovision Star Sandie Jones with the Dixies. Sandie had the honour of singing 'Ceol an Grá', the only time Ireland had a song 'as gaeilge' in the Eurovision Song Contest!

With Monday being the musicians' day off, things like recreation, getting your hair cut or 'getting married' always took place on a Monday. So, fair play to Shamie Curran and the lads in the 'Terrific Pacific' who organised a kick-around on Monday afternoons for the 'stars' to meet up and shoot the breeze! This usually took place behind the Star Cinema in Crumlin, hence the name. Back row: The Ref, Dermot O'Brien, Mel Austin (Casino), Dave Pennyfeather (Real McCoy), Mick (Shamrock Rovers). Front row: Jimmy Higgins (Millionaires), Brendan Carroll (Cadets), Gregory (Cadets), Sonny Knowles (Pacific), John Woodful (Casino/Indians). The opposition were afraid to turn up for the photograph!

This photograph of the Celebration Band, with the man who would later become Taoiseach, Mr. Albert Reynolds, was taken at the Corrib Great Southern Hotel in Galway c. 1992/3. Most of us would have played for Albert and his brothers down through the years in their well-known chain of ballrooms throughout the country – Dreamland in Athy, Roseland in Moate, Lakeland in Mullingar, Barrowland in New Ross etc. As a fourteen-year-old I played with The Paramount in their first ballroom, the Cloudland in Rooskey. I was very impressed with the lighting effects as they changed from clouds to starry skies! We were the support act for Mick Mulligan's Jazzband, featuring the great George Melly on vocals. Line-up from left: John Merrick, Carl Hession, Joe Bernie, Jimmy Reilly, Fergal Gallagher, Jimmy Higgins. Albert Reynolds, Mags Heffernan, vocalist.

opportunity to visit the major cities of the UK, the US and Canada. While a trip to London was always nice with the chance to see some soccer or music shows, I have to say, without doubt, that nothing compared to the American tour. The chance to experience that big, bright, brash American culture was always a great adventure to look forward to. I considered it to be one of the great perks of the game; the opportunity to see faraway places, having your expenses paid and getting gig money as well. Where would you get it? Brilliant!

The US tours were usually centred round the major cities of the east coast: New York, Boston, Philadelphia and Chicago. We would play in the many Irish clubs that catered for the strong Irish population of those regions. Some of the bigger bands like The Royal or The Cadets would travel to San Francisco on the west coast.

Expo '67

As an add-on to our US tour of 1967, it was arranged that we'd play for a weekend at the Maple Leaf ballroom in Toronto before travelling on to the US for the usual circuit of Boston, New York, Chicago and Philadelphia. The massive world trade fair known as Expo '67 was in full swing in Montreal where we had a few hours stop on our way to Toronto. As we couldn't leave the airport, there was nothing else to do except scout around the shops which of course were just flooded with souvenirs of the Expo. I spotted some suit covers, plastic ones, with the Expo logo emblazoned on them. I convinced our manager Johnny to buy a set for the band and we could use them to hype up the tour by saying what a great success we had been at Expo '67 in Montreal.

We didn't even get to see the Expo, let alone play at it. By the time we got home after touring for four weeks, the cheap plastic blue and white suit covers were beginning to fall apart. So much for the 'big publicity stunt', how desperate can you get? Still, you know what they say, God loves a trier.

When we arrived at Toronto we had the usual hassle about visas but we fobbed it off by saying we thought that Canada and the US had the same emigration system. Sure, weren't we only young lads after flying from Ireland and landing in Canada for the first time, but we'd have it all fixed up properly the next time we came over. Anyway, we were only staying for a few days and we would be gone out of their way again on Monday, off to New York. What could they do but let us through? So far, so good, but I'm afraid our luck was to change a little when we arrived at the Maple Leaf Ballroom to set up the gear and do a sound check.

On this occasion we had decided to bring our own PA with us and, as we set up the main amplifier, we noticed two valves had been smashed in transit. Major panic stations, it was about 4pm so we had to move fast. We chatted with one of the guys at the venue and he took Johnny and myself to an electrical store to try and get some replacements.

'Have you any EL42 valves for a dynachord amp?' we said to the storekeeper.

'Did you say valves? No, we don't have any valve things.'

Unfortunately, we hadn't thought of taking one of the valves that was still intact with us to show him. I was watching the clock, it was close on 5.30pm and shops closed at 6pm, so it was too late to try another place. We started to look around in desperation and I spotted some brown boxes on the top shelf that looked a lot like the cartons the valves came in when we bought them from Hurley's at home in Dublin. I asked your man if we could have a look at what was in the box on the top shelf and when he opened it up, what do you think was inside? Only the EL42!

'That's what we were looking for,' said I excitedly.

'Them's tubes,' he said. 'Why didn't you say tubes in the first place?'

'Oh yeah, I must remember that for the next time. Anyway, give us four of them before ye close.'

Talk about the devil's boy having the devil's luck, another close shave with a PA. Testing, testing, one, two, three?

Entertainment Gargle
In those days, the mid Sixties, the duty-free allowance to the States went something like this. Tourist allowance was five bottles, US resident two bottles. As The Millionaires were regular visitors (we toured for one month each year) we got to know the drill.

A bottle of Irish whisky was always a welcome gift from home for our relatives or friends in the States. Others would be thrilled with Irish rashers, Taytos, Crunchies, Lucozade and other similar treats from the old country. We were all instructed, even non-drinkers, to avail of the full quota of five bottles of duty free and then each guy donated one bottle of liquor to the kitty known as the 'entertainment gargle'. This kitty was closely managed by the 'Bilser' (our trombone player, Billy Doyle) and yours truly. Whenever there was a party organised, we would have a whip-around of a few dollars per man to cover the cost of beer and other niceties like crisps, sambos or pizzas.

Our New York base was the Woodward Hotel (affectionately known as the Woodworm). This was on the corner of West 55th and Broadway, within walking distance of the City Centre ballroom, the major Irish venue in New York run by Bill Fuller.

The tour would usually open and close with a few nights at the City Centre in New York, with trips to the other major Irish strongholds like Boston, Chicago, Philadelphia, Cleveland and San Francisco spread through the middle weekends. After the opening weekend in New York, you wouldn't be due to play again until the following Friday in, say, Boston or Chicago, so you could take three days to get there or, as we preferred, go directly to the next city and spend your free days having a look around the city and getting to as many music venues as possible. We usually travelled by road under the gentle care of Big Tony Monaghan from Belmullet. Tony was our roadie and minder and, for those of us not used to such luxuries at home, this was a real treat. He was like a father or favourite uncle to us and when we got to Chicago, his American home town, he pulled out all the stops.

On one occasion travelling from New York to Chicago, which we were trying to pull off in a direct trip, the weather turned so bad we had to dock at Buffalo and stay at a motel.

When we got back into the wagon the next morning everything was frozen solid, including a few bottles of coke and soda we had left lying around. In fact, the bottles had actually cracked where the ice had expanded overnight. Tony was explaining that it was so many degrees below freezing when the 'Conn' (Mickey Connolly) chipped in, 'Yeah, I thought as much when I heard the brass monkeys speaking in high-pitched voices!'

The wagon was one of those four rows of seats jobs, twice as long as what we were used to back in Ireland, with all the gear on the roofrack overhead. The boys decided to stash the beer there as well, and every so often you'd hear a request for a beer from the 'cooler' overhead. Some choice language would follow as the window was opened to reach the fridge and the bitter cold air rushed in and proceeded to freeze the 'Harry Halls' off the passengers.

On eventually arriving in the cold and windy city of Chicago, we went straight to a popular Irish pub called O'Neill's where some friends had gathered to welcome us. As we were more than a few hours late some of the party had dispersed while some others were a little worse for wear, but this did not stop them from giving us a big welcome.

O'Neill's was well known for its Irish music sessions and there were regular broadcasts from the venue on local radio. After a few hours of an Irish welcome there, it was time to check into the hotel and get settled for a few days. The visiting bands usually stayed at the Phillip's Motel on South Cicero, so when we pulled into the parking area we were surprised to find the place in darkness. But not for long! Before one of us even had time to get out of the wagon to check out the situation, we were surrounded by four cop cars with lights flashing all over the place.

'Christ, what's happening?' We thought we were all going to be shot.

'Relax!' shouted Big Tony. 'Let me handle this.'

And surprise, surprise nobody objected. 'Sure, Tony, you just go ahead.'

As a few of the cops approached the bus, Tony lowered his window gently and greeted them in his best Mayo accent. 'What seems to be the problem officer?' he asked.

'Can I see your licence, sir?' asked the cop as Tony was already reaching into the glove compartment for it, while at the same time carefully stuffing a few dollars between the pages. The cop opens the licence book, smoothly slips the money into his pocket without a word, takes a look at the licence, mutters something to the effect that everything seems to be in order and proceeds to ask us what we were doing there. Tony explains that we were a band on tour from Ireland and were due to stay here as usual, when the cop informs us that the place had been closed a few days earlier by the state authority.

It was supposed to have been run by the Mafia. He advised us to move on and try one of the other motels locally. With that, Tony requested a bottle of Irish from the kitty in the back and, after a few groans from Billy and a few grunts from Tony to hurry up, he handed the cop the bottle telling him it was a little present from Ireland to share with his officer friends. We hightailed it out of there as fast as we could to find a safer house. As the flashing blue beacon of the squad cars faded in our wing mirrors, we breathed sighs of relief, happy with the fact that we were all still in one piece.

How Many Drummers Does It Take To Do A Gig?
Most of the venues had resident bands, based on the showband style, with as many Irish guys as possible playing the usual Top 20 chart hits with a bit of Irish thrown in. The unions were always strong in the States so when Irish bands were visiting, the local

musicians' union would monitor the line-up so as to arrange pairings if necessary, just like in Dáil Éireann.

There was one scenario in the city centre in New York where the resident band was only a five-piece and we had a seven-piece plus a manager. The union sent along three musicians and they sat alongside the stage while the resident band played. As soon as we took over to play for the remainder of the night, the three boys got paid their fee from the leader of the resident band and headed home. This procedure was repeated each night we played that venue, as this was the union agreement with live venues. We were all happy to see the live musician being protected and supported which was the objective of the arrangement.

We chatted with the guys over the few nights and I remember one of them saying to us, 'Hey you Irish guys got it made, all you gotta do is stand up there and whistle and you go over a storm.'

The fact that the lads (deputies) were three drummers added another bit of spice to the story. How many drummers does it take to play a gig? One in the resident band, one in the visiting band, one retired drummer (our manager) plus the three deputies sent in by the union makes six. Even if we did just whistle and sing, I'd still feel better about it than putting my hand out for money after sitting on my bum all night!

Cassius Clay (Muhammad Ali)

During the US tour of October 1964 we got to meet the great Cassius Clay. He was in Boston, training for his world championship bout with Sonny Liston, and we heard that his training camp was close to where we were staying. So, we got the opportunity to watch him train and have photographs taken with the great man. He was only 22 or 23 years of age at the time and was very polite and rather shy.

The training sessions were open to the public for a small admission fee, so most of the band went along to see him. Our guitar player Paul, who was English, had a small cinecamera and was filming Cassius as he sparred with Jimmy Ellis. Angelo Dundee, Clay's trainer, was moving about the place and he came over to Paul and said, 'I hope you're not spying for the Liston camp.'

Paul explained we were a band on tour and asked if it would be possible to meet the 'champ' later. Dundee said he'd see what he could do. Sure enough, when the session ended, they announced over the PA that everybody had to leave except the press and the 'British group'. After a little while, Cassius came out to meet the press and ourselves and he was very polite and stood around for photos.

He had met with The Beatles a short time before we met him, and he asked, 'Do you guys know The Beatles? They're great friends of mine.'

I have seen some great photographs of Clay messing about in the ring with The Beatles. Later he asked, 'Which of you guys is the singer?' and continued to proclaim, 'I'm a singer too.' He had, in fact, recorded a version of 'Up On The Roof' with his own song 'I'm The Greatest' on the flipside.

He was very courteous and laid back. However, a few days later we saw him on television as he and Sonny Liston arrived for the pre-fight weigh-in. Clay had a rope and a jar of honey and he was running after Liston's car shouting, 'I'm gonna catch the big ugly bear.' It was all an act to get maximum publicity to help sell tickets for the fight. That's showbiz folks!

As it happened, Clay injured himself in training that week and the fight had to be postponed for a few months, but he still beat Liston when they eventually met. We were very disappointed, as we were planning to fly from New York to Boston to see the fight. It was around this time that he changed his name from Cassius Clay to Muhammad Ali and when I got his autograph, he signed it 'Muhammad Ali'. In my innocence, thinking that nobody would know who this was, I wrote underneath, '(Cassius Clay)'.

Visas and Passports

They were always a nuisance. We always had problems because we were without visas. We just never seemed to have any organised. When I think back on it now, the possible root to visa problems was that we were trying to travel on visitors' visas as they were easier to acquire. We were also trying to avoid having to declare earnings which meant making tax returns for a short period of three to four weeks. Realistically, we wouldn't generate a lot of revenue for the taxman as the money was never great on these tours when you took all the costs of travel and accommodation into account.

Not that we were complaining. As I said earlier, the thrill we got out of the trips to the States was brilliant because we were treated like stars by everybody, the promoters and punters alike. People couldn't do enough for us. I remember friends taking time off work to bring us sightseeing and inviting the whole band out to their homes for dinner as well as giving us presents when we were going home. People were so decent and generous that sometimes it was embarrassing, because middle-of-the-road bands weren't used to being treated like that. Of course, we lapped it up.

They used to tell us that they were so pleased to see bands from home because in the mid-Sixties only about six or eight bands would visit each year. In those days people would only return home on holiday every five or maybe ten years. It was a sign of their loneliness for home, the way they would identify with a certain band or also when football or hurling teams would travel over.

In 1964, while I was based in England working with The International, I remember having to organise my passport in London for our trip to Germany in 1964. Then later that year, before travelling to the US, we had to make arrangements with the musicians' union in Manchester for clearance to work in the States. I remember this lovely little English gentleman in the office showing us the forms he had arranged for a Liverpool group who had recently returned from a tour of the States, The Beatles. He wished us well and hoped we would have similar success. If only!

Mayor Daly

While in the States every opportunity was availed of to promote the band. If the tour was during Lent and you were there for St Patrick's Day, a huge day in the life of the Irish community, then bands were encouraged to take part in the parade.

In 1966, The Millionaires met Mayor Daly in Chicago and in 1969, The Raindrops met Mayor Kevin White of Boston to present him with the inevitable piece of Galway Crystal, any excuse for a photograph.

When the long hairstyle became fashionable some of the bands were greeted with scowls from the clean-cut American folk. Some bands were told to get their hair cut, that they were a disgrace to Ireland.

When The Raindrops were invited to join the parade in south Boston in 1969, we all dressed up in our best mohair suits only to find that we were the only people not wearing something green. We were driven around in an open-top limo at a snail's pace and whenever we passed a politician's house they would load some beer into our limo. This must have been the Boston version of 'give the band more porter'! There were over 200 floats in that parade and we were second last, how exciting!

Touring abroad had a multi-purpose benefit, the obvious one being that it provided a few weeks of valuable work, especially if it happened during a quiet time at home like Lent. However, another benefit was that it could be treated as a kind of holiday and yet another was that it was a great vehicle for publicity.

The idea was to get your photograph taken with everyone or anything that would pass for a celebrity. They could be a sports star, film star, musician, politician, policeman or fireman. Even a cardboard cut-out of someone famous like Donald Duck or Lassie would do. Every photo opportunity was availed of – high profile shots and stimulating information like us getting on the plane or us getting off the plane. That kind of stuff!

Ten
Towards the End

Bawnboy

I t's New Year's Eve 1979, early afternoon, and as we're preparing to travel tonight to Bawnboy in Cavan, I notice that it's just started to snow. I know from experience that if it's snowing in Galway, where we're usually not hit too badly because we're beside the sea, as we travel north it will get worse. We leave about 5pm, collecting the guys along the way, ending up with six guys in the Volkswagen van and a trailer behind with all the gear. As we travel through the towns of north Galway, Tuam, Dunmore and on towards Roscommon, the snow is coming down thick and fast. We know we're in for a bit of a rough ride, just to get to the gig.

What it's going to be like when we get there is another question. It has already crossed my mind a few times as to whether I made the right decision by not accepting Danny Doyle's 'poor offer' of a straight fee of £250 to play down in

Wexford. It's New Year's Eve, the biggest night of the year, everyone's going to have a big crowd, so it seemed to make sense to take this big offer of a 50/50 percentage deal for the gig in Bawnboy.

As we motor on up through Roscommon and into Longford, heading in the general direction of Cavan, the weather is bad and seems to be getting worse. I know it will be dangerous with the trailer skidding down that steep hill into Ballinagh and along to Granard. Bawnboy is quite near Ballyconnell which is right on the border.

About 15 miles from the gig, as we turned onto a secondary road, there was just one big blanket of snow and we couldn't distinguish between the middle of the road and the middle of a field. Up until then we had been lucky enough that there had been some traffic on the road before us so we had a kind of guideline in the shape of two mucky lines through the snow. But it was quite obvious no traffic had been on this secondary road for some time. We trundled along and, as we were going up a hill which wasn't too steep, we began to skid, our biggest fear. The van started to slip back down the hill and we knew we were in trouble. With the trailer on tow you have no control so the inevitable happened – it skidded backwards into the ditch, almost pulling the rear of the van in with it. Luckily, only the trailer went in fully, which was bad enough as all our gear was in it.

Anyway, we must have been around ten miles from the gig and it was well after 10pm at this stage. What were we going to do? I started to walk in the direction of Bawnboy, hoping that somebody would come along and give me a lift. Eventually, somebody did. It was a priest, the local curate, and he too was heading for a gig, a disco in Ballyconnell. He was running it for the Youth Club and he had all the gear, records and record player, in the back seat. So, being the Christian man he was, he took pity on me even though I was supposed to be his main opposition for the night as Ballyconnell was only about five miles from Bawnboy. He gave me a lift and dropped me off quite near the local ballroom which was adjacent to a pub. I thanked him and he headed away.

I looked around me. There were a few cars outside the pub but my eye was caught by one beautiful machine – a tractor! In I go to the half-empty bar, very conscious that I was right beside the border and these were troubled times when strangers would be viewed with suspicion. There was some shuffling at the bar and a few heads half-turned to look at me, so I mustered up my broadest west of Ireland accent as I headed towards the barman to proclaim to nobody in particular, 'I'm with the band and we are broken down back the road. The trailer has gone into the ditch and we're in an awful state. Could you organise any help? Does anyone know who owns the tractor outside?'

Or words to that effect! After a few mumblings and mutterings, a fella slid off a stool and nodded his head in the direction of the door. I assumed he had decided he would come and help us, so I followed him out. He loaded me onto the tractor and we went back the road to where the lads were. First of all, he pulled the trailer out of the ditch. Then he latched it up to the van and proceeded to pull van and trailer, lads and all, the last few miles to the gig.

At this stage, it was close to 11.30pm and, as one of the main functions on a New Year's Eve was to play a bit of music before midnight to welcome in the New Year, there was a mad scramble to get the gear in and organised. Some of us changed into our uniforms but others didn't bother and we started to play with five minutes to spare because we were afraid the 'crowd' would get restless. At this stage there were at most four people in the hall. In fact there were exactly four people in the hall because I counted them and that was all that came for the whole night. We played two tunes; welcomed in the New Year and then played two more tunes (one for each person in the hall) before deciding to cut our losses.

We called it off at that stage. Two of the lads who were in the hall came up, and one looked at us with a glint in his eye and asked, 'Was it something we said?'

So there you have it, four people, four tunes. Of course, we wished everybody a happy and prosperous New Year, including ourselves, and just to keep the statistics in mind: 50 per cent of nothing is nothing, so we got our 50 per cent for our trouble and hard travelling up to Bawnboy.

I will always remember looking down the hall and saying to myself, 'Yeah, this is the year of the big decision. I am going to pack it in.'

I could see it going downhill from there on in. Did I say downhill? Surely it couldn't get much lower than that? Four punters?

Kinnegad

Later that year, there was another sort of a minor incident while we were playing in Kinnegad. You see, up to then all the halls were what we called 'dry' halls. In other words, they had no alcoholic bars. But this venue in Kinnegad did have a licence as it must have been attached to a hotel. The punters were drinking from plastic glasses. Discos had become popular at this stage and you would often have one supporting you. I remember they had these new lighting projectors which created a completely different atmosphere. The main lights in the halls were kept low, making the place darker to facilitate the new atmospheric enhancer, the disco lights. While the DJ played non-stop background music before the band, most of the dancers would be in the bar drinking as the disco gathered momentum, churning out this non-stop conveyor belt music.

So, when the 'live' band arrived on stage it then had to try and compete with this 'non stop music' policy and keep the music going. You must remember the old system was to play a set of dances, which would be three tunes, and then you would say, 'We'll continue dancing with a slow waltz.' You would play three waltzes, followed by a set of quick-steps and then maybe a slow foxtrot and so on, with each set of three tunes concluded by the MC saying, 'That's all for now, your next dance please.'

The purpose of all this was to let the dancers know that you'd finished that particular set of dancing. Then, when you would announce a waltz, the people who preferred waltzing would get up. You see, some people had a preference for the slow tunes while others preferred the fast. But with the advent of the disco, all of this changed, it was non-stop. While the DJ just kept playing records, the people got up and danced whenever they felt like it and when they got fed-up, they sat down. So, a band might be into the second or third tune of the 'set' when people started to dance and then when you announced the end of the set, they would be looking at you and saying, 'What the hell is wrong with you? We only got up.'

They may have only got up but other dancers might have been up for the last ten minutes. You had to run one thing into another and the days of the different 'sets' were nearly gone. The point was that the only time they looked up was when you stopped playing, in other words if there was a power failure or something happened and you had to stop. Then they would stand there with a 'what's wrong with ye?' expression.

Something like this happened as I had the trumpet up to my lips. The next thing, I felt this slop of beer across my jaw. Some boyo was finished with his beer and decided he would just throw the glass at us. Luckily it was only a plastic glass, but the dregs of beer from the bottom slapped across my jaw as the glass flew past.

It was a somewhat defining moment in my musical career as I asked myself, 'Do I really like being here doing this? What am I here for? Job satisfaction? Improving my musical ability? Or am I like the Kerry jazz musician, just in it for the money? Unfortunately it's because I have to do it, as this is my job.'

There was another moment of truth: 'Is this where I want to be?'

On the positive side, I suppose I should consider myself lucky that he wasn't drinking out of a bucket! But it was time to reconsider the terms and conditions of my career. Maybe I should apply for danger money. At least if I were a drinker, I could have licked my jaw!

Donegal – The Last Straw

Later again that year, in September, we were playing in Donegal on a Saturday and Seapoint on the Sunday. On the following Tuesday, we were to leave for England for a ten-day tour at the end of which we were taking our annual holidays before heading into the winter season. So, the Saturday was Donegal and I remember passing through Tuam and we were waiting in The Square to pick up Walty.

The bould Jarlath Moloney came along in the car and we had a bit of a slag and a laugh. Jarlath said, 'Going to Donegal? Oh, I'd hate that.'

He didn't know how much I was dreading it because I was having trouble with my back at the time. Anyway, we headed off for Donegal and when we eventually arrived at the gig, after what would have been a good five hours travelling in the Volkswagen, I was bent over for 20 minutes before I could straighten up.

So, there I was stretching and trying to stand up, about to go for the bite to eat and I said to myself, 'Definitely this is the last long journey I want to do in Ireland.'

I got straightened out, had something to eat, played the gig and travelled back home. The next night we were playing in Seapoint and I was feeling the pits. I literally had the bell of the trumpet left on the microphone. I don't like playing directly into a microphone (it's just against the nature of the training) but because of the volume of noise, guitars and drums, you have to play towards a microphone. But this night I had the bell resting on the microphone; I hadn't the strength to blow out.

The next day, Monday, I fainted in the kitchen. When I woke up, my wife was rubbing a wet cloth on my face. There I was, on the floor in the kitchen. The following day I went to the doctor and was sent straight to hospital. There was no way I was going to England so I didn't even have the pleasure of finishing with a tour. It was decided for me.

I was in hospital on the Wednesday as the lads were heading off on their tour of England. A last minute substitute was drafted in for me, but he was really there to go through the motions. Unfortunately, that was how I finished on the road as a full-time musician. I spent a couple of weeks 'on vacation' in Merlin Park Hospital and while I was there I remember being woken early one morning by a nurse and saying to her, 'Oh, thank God, this is where I am! I was dreaming I was on a tour of England!'

Eleven
Memories I Just Can't Erase

Where Do I Begin?

1956 was a year that was to leave a lasting impression on me as a ten-year-old youngster. It was the year that Galway won the All Ireland football final and I remember being in the Square in Tuam to welcome home the team with the Sam Maguire Cup. They were led by three Tuam men: captain Jack Mangan and 'the terrible twins', Sean Purcell and Frankie Stockwell. It was also the year that Russian tanks rolled into Budapest resulting in a young classical trumpeter named Joe Chebi getting out and moving west to eventually settle in Dublin where he worked for many years as principal trumpet with the National Symphony Orchestra. Also, on 1 December 1956, Ronnie Delaney won an Olympic gold medal for Ireland in Melbourne. But, most importantly for me, 1956 was the year that I joined the Tuam Brass and Reed Band.

I started in the drum section but was delighted when, after a few months, I was moved to the trumpet section! Unlike a lot of provincial towns, Tuam was fortunate in having a musical teacher of the calibre of bandmaster Mr Danny Kelly in its midst. Although small in stature, this musical maestro had a huge impact on the lives of the youngsters who were lucky enough to attend his classes over the years. He produced some fine players, and it was no great surprise to see that many of them went on to play with some of the top bands in the country including the Army and Garda bands.

I don't know if the same applied to all instrumentalists, but I found that whenever I went to see another band I would always pay a little extra attention to the brass and especially the trumpet player. Sometimes, you'd be in awe of a particular player, while on another occasion you'd feel, 'yeah, I could handle that.'

Of course, if you were to hear the odd fluffed note you could relax a bit in the knowledge that you weren't alone and that the other lads were human as well. I often wondered if it was the same with all the other guys, that we were all taking part in this unofficial competition with each other or was it only just going on in my head? Come on now lads, out with it!

So, let's say hello to some of the lads – the opposition:

Ollie Maloney [Johnny Flynn, Ohio], Billy Kelly [Swingtimes, Johnny Flynn], Tommy Walshe [Nevada, Graduates], Gerry Mulryan [Gentry, Red Hurley], Martin Hynes [Fleet, Ohio], Eamonn Mangan [Ohio], Tommy Ward [Ollie Maloney], Eddie Sullivan [Royal], Johnny Carroll [Premiers, Magic], Bobby Smyth [Royal Blues], Frankie McDonald [Drifters], Judd Ruane [Jack Ruane], Tommy Bourke [Big 8], Paul Sweeney [Capitol], Marco Petrassi [Jim Farley], Bram McCarthy [Capitol], Earl Gill

[Hoedowners], Hugo Quinn [Clippers], Mike Nolan [D O'Brien], Patsy Haugh [Riviera, Johnny Flynn], Emmett Wynne [Airchords], Brian Wynne [Gloria, Top 7], Tommy Swarbrigg [Drifters, Times], Eamonn Keane [Casino, Indians], Sean Mahon [Freshmen], Dave Coady [Real McCoy, Big 8], Ray Moore [Plattermen, Paddy Cole] George Hasson [Trixons], Frank McCaffrey [Country Folk].

Over the past few years I have been lucky enough to play alongside some fine players during my stints with Galway's Black Magic Band and Gerry Macken's Big Band. Players like Shay Nolan, John Merrick, Frank Donlon, John Fleming, Keith McDonald and that 'boy wonder' who has turned out to be one of the finest players this country has ever produced, the brilliant Danny Healy.

Unfortunately, some of the aforementioned 'heads' have passed on and are now enjoying an eternal bugler's holiday. We pray that the good Lord will be generous to them all.

The Best of the Rest (The Best in the West)
As I write this, I am listening to the great Americn trumpeter Al Hirt in the background and the stuff he's coming out with would put the hair standing on the back of your neck. One of the tunes he just played was called 'Sugar Lips', so with that I'll give a respectful nod in the direction of one of my trumpet playing heroes, Ireland's Louis Armstrong, Tuam's one and only, Mr Ollie Maloney.

'How'm I blowin', Sham?' he'd say to one of his many admiring fans. 'Can ya hear me alright down the back?' As if he needed to ask!

One night, as we were discussing some new kid on the block, he said to me, 'Ah, he's good, I'll grant you that, but I'll tell ya one thing Sham, he's not great! He hasn't got the blasht!'

'And do you know what?' he went on, 'I think he was trying to impress me. God bless his innocence, sure I've forgotten more than he'll ever learn.'

When the local choirmaster inquired as to whether he could read musical arrangements for a classical choral piece, the great man was heard to say, 'Read music is it? Sham, I could read wallpaper.'

As a new drummer was watching Ollie warm up, he noticed that he stopped every so often to tighten his false teeth and straighten his 'thatch'. 'Sounds great,' said the drummer, slightly in awe of the maestro.

Ollie winks at him and says, 'Not bad Sham, for a guy who's all spare parts.'

Higgins Brothers of Athenry Road, Tuam

I come from a family of six children – three boys and three girls. All of the boys took to the music but none of the girls (Marie, Eileen or Loretta) did. However, Mary Robinson would have been delighted with them because all three of them would 'dance for Ireland'. And so they did – mainly in the west of Ireland I suppose!

Having received a good grounding in the brass band, the three boys progressed to the showband scene, with yours truly leading the way!

Francie learned the tenor sax and hit the road with The Problems. From there he moved to The Swingtime Aces, The

Raindrops, and The Big Time before eventually trading the sax for a disco set-up. Sadly he passed away suddenly in 1998.

Paddy's versatility on the drums/vocals enabled him to travel the world successfully with various bands including Liam Ivory, The Raindrops, Eileen Reid, Dermot Henry and The Virginians, Margo and the Country Folk and Dermot Hegarty. He spent many years in New York with Christy O'Connor before going to Las Vegas with Brendan Bowyer. Paddy still enjoys playing on the American circuit!

Celebrity

Like politicians, most showband musicians were always on the lookout for a publicity stunt. We had no shame when it came to our quest for fame, so any photo opportunity that came our way was not to be missed. And bear in mind that from where I was standing, almost everybody was a celebrity.

Here's a quick look at my brush with the famous:

Admiring Margaret Barry's banjo in Ballindine in 1960, my introduction to fame. Listening to George Melly sing about his 'Black Bottom' in the Cloudland in Rooskey. Rocking the night away in the Las Vegas ballroom in Sligo with Adam Faith.

Partying with Clodagh Rodgers at the 32 Club in Harlesden in London. Clubbing with Millie and Freddie Starr in Hamburg. Working 'close' to Paul McCartney. We were only a few feet away from him as we packed our gear into the van outside the Blarney in Tottenham Court Road in London. As the lights were red, he had stopped alongside us in his Jag. When the lights changed he gave us a little wave as he sped off into the night. Recognition at last!

All smiles with Cassius Clay, Mayors Daly of Chicago and Kevin White of Boston. Tea with Judith Durham of The Seekers in a little house across from the ballroom in Blackrock, County Louth. Early breakfast at 4am somewhere on the M1 motorway with Kenny Ball. Sounding out Sandie Shaw in the Atlantic in Tramore as I acted as her soundman. Waiting for Dusty Springfield for almost two hours before she came on stage to perform for less than an hour at the Crystal in Dublin. She then headed off after midnight to Mullingar for a second gig!

Hanging out backstage with Tom Waites at the Late Late Show studios in RTÉ. And I not having a clue who he was.

Serving Sting in my Music City record shop when he came in to buy a tape of U2. Their manager was pestering him to use them as support band for The Police gig in Leixlip. He must have liked the tape. Which reminds me, I never received any royalties from Bono and de boys! Nuttin, not even a rusty bicycle.

Odds and Ends

Travelling home at night in a draughty van trying to keep warm in the days before sleeping bags. One of the tricks was to have an old overcoat where you could put your legs into the sleeves. This, however could cause major havoc when someone would shout, 'Put a hump on the wagon or stick her to the tar, I want to have a leak!'

Then, when people weren't fully awake there was always the danger of leaving someone behind in the dark of the night as did happen to a band from Tipperary who 'lost' one of the lads in the middle of Mayo at 4am. And this was before mobile phones, so it certainly was 'a long way to Tipperary' for someone.

On another occasion, as a band were refuelling at a filling station, one of the lads decided he'd like an ice cream. You can imagine his shock when he arrived back to find the van had gone off without him. As the rest of the guys had been sleeping, no one missed him so he had to make his own way home.

God help the poor unsuspecting punter who would thumb a lift in a band-wagon. We had a variety of pranks, like everybody would start singing or whistling a different tune. Or we'd give a nice choral version of 'Newtownmountkennedy' to the air of 'Donna Et Mobile', all five verses. Sometimes, we'd just give them the 'silent' treatment, nobody would speak and we'd all pretend to have various twitches.

That great wizard of the accordion, Liam Ivory, when asked what a gig was like, once replied, 'The feckin' crowd were so dry they were farting dust!'

'Put on the blower quick, the Bilser's after releasing a porter fart that would waken the dead.' If we could only bottle it and sell it as poison gas.

Access All Areas

One Christmas night, when Magic and the Swallows were playing the Ranch House in Cummer, the crowd was so large that their guitar player couldn't get in. So, the promoter took him around the back of the hall, where he removed a panel to allow him access to the back of the stage. When you're big, you're big.

A fiddle player who liked to have everything organised on time arrived for a gig in County Clare, set up his gear, tuned up and headed off to the pub for a quiet pint. On his arrival back at the venue, he found another band on stage playing and his gear pushed into a corner. When he checked with the organiser, he realised that his band were playing at another venue about 20 miles away.

Food

Getting a bit of grub before a gig sometimes became a big problem. On one occasion we arrived in north Donegal after travelling from Dublin and when we went for the meal provided, we were given beans on toast, one slice each. We decided to look for something more substantial downtown only to find, when we asked a local woman, that there was no café or restaurant in the place. She had great pity for us, so when one of the lads asked her if we bought some food would she cook it for us, she said, 'Of course I will.' So, after a quick visit to the local butcher, the seven hungry musicians were soon tucking into a beautiful fry of bacon, egg and sausages. Fair play to that generous woman and yes, we did give her a photograph of the band and a few bob for her trouble.

Another time we were travelling from Galway again to the top of Donegal, a journey that was the best part of 200 miles as we had to go through Derry to get there. When the gig finished at 2am, we ordered tea and sandwiches to sustain us on the long journey home. When the gear was packed and the sambos devoured, I went to collect our fee and was told we were being deducted £3 for the refreshments. I was given the balance which was £32! I put the money in my pocket, hopped into the Ford Transit, which had a full tank of petrol, and we headed for Galway, hoping that we wouldn't be ambushed along the way with all that cash on board. After about five hours driving on a terrible stormy night, we were within six miles of home, when we ran out of petrol.

Yes, that's right, a full tank of petrol was not enough to take us home, the gig was that far away. So, out we got, locked up the trusty old Transit, and seven sleepy showband stars started thumbing the last few miles home. It was a Sunday morning, and as I walked up my street with my trumpet case, I was meeting people going to Mass and I'm sure some of them were saying, 'Look at that fella and he only coming home now, isn't it well for some people?'

By the way, seven into 32, how much is that each? Oh sorry, I forgot about the petrol, ahhh, give me back a pound each there, lads. Yeah, the price of fame is steep all right.

Another 'meal for the band story', but this time in County Cork, just to give Donegal a break. It was a marquee gig in a small village, so as usual we had set up the equipment before being directed to the appointed house which had the misfortune of looking after the hungry bunch of musicians. It was a lovely country cottage and we were shown into the front room where the table was beautifully laid out. At the time, two of our boys were guests on the TV Show, *Hoedown*, which also featured Sean Dunphy and Earl Gill. The family seemed to be very excited about having some TV stars in the house, whatever about the rest of us. As it was summer time, the meal was obviously going to be a salad, sandwiches and tea. There seemed to be a few teenage daughters in the family because every time anyone asked for more tea, a different daughter came in to pour for us, such service. The family could not have been nicer, with the parents and girls all chatting and asking for signed photographs. It was wonderful.

However, the one little downer was that the salad sandwiches weren't great, they only contained scallions, you know those thin little green onions. As we were taking our leave and shaking hands with them all and thanking them for their hospitality, I hear one of the lads who was coming behind me saying, 'Cheerio, and thanks very much for the grass sandwiches.'

Christ, I nearly died with embarrassment, and needless to say your man got an earful when we got into the van! As they say, 'You can dress them up, but you can't leave them on their own.'

Are Miki Conn and Joe Doherty really twins? Some punters would actually ask that.

Mickey Conn and Joe Doherty were the yodelling twins of The Millionaires and stars of *Hoedown*. They appeared every week alongside Sean Dunphy, Earl Gill and Rose Tynan. Joe recorded a song called 'Chyme Bells' that had this long note which we used as a type of show stopper where I used to make a big deal with the punters about timing this long note. In fact, I remember when my watch was actually stopped for a few weeks but this didn't stop me from continuing with the charade about the 'longest note ever recorded', broken watch or not.

Recording

Bearing in mind the cost of studio time, bands would try their best to memorise their tunes to avoid expensive rehearsals in the studio. However, things didn't always work out according to plan. On one such occasion, when there seemed to be a lot of delays in between takes, the manager, who was watching the clock, asked the lads what was the cause of all the delays.

'We don't have the right chords for the tune,' he was told.

'Well,' he replied, 'Ye're earning enough money now, why don't ye buy some new ones?'

His reply was typical of a manager who didn't have a note in his head. The only notes some of them knew or cared about were pound notes. The 'dartboard' school of management type!

Identity Crisis

'Who are we tonight?' asked one of the lads when he noticed the band leader stopping every hour or so to paint over the name on the van on the way to a gig. Having a band called after the bandleader was old fashioned so bands were being re-christened overnight by changing the name from Paddy Murphy's Band to something like High Society, Larry and the Lookalikes, Willie and the Wannabees, or Sheila and the Shockers.

Craving Success

If only something major would have happened to us, like having a hit record or winning the Eurovision. Jaysus, even to be runner-up in the Cavan or Castlebar song contest would have done us, we weren't fussy. What about if the van were to accidentally catch fire? Surely, we'd get loads of publicity and sympathy out of that.

The Hard Luck Story

There was always someone or something holding us back. Either the singer was too small or the manager was no good, or maybe it was because we had the wrong type of echo unit, like our homemade neon sign on top of the van.

It was a real case of 'Dear Mr Atlas, as I have now completed the course, would you please send on the muscles.' We have the red suits and speakers like The Royal, a van and mikes like The Capitol, and play most of The Dixies' songs. We're ready, so what's the big delay with our success?

What's keeping ye?

Memo To Budding Stars

Be nice to people on the way up because you'll meet them again on the way down. Only when that time comes you'll be travelling twice as fast!

'Who are we? We're the band, where's the gargle?'

Would we do it all again?

Of course we would. Sure, weren't we nearly famous?

That's all for now folks, your next dance please.

Appendix I
Eurovision Song Contest

Year	Performer	Title/Writers	Place
1965	Butch Moore	I'm Walking the Streets in the Rain *by Teresa Conlon, George Prendergast and Joe Harrison*	6th
1966	Dickie Rock	Come Back To Stay *by Rowland Soper*	4th
1967	Sean Dunphy	If I Could Choose *by Wesley Burrowes and Michael Coffey*	2nd
1968	Pat McGeegan	Chance of a Lifetime *by John Kennedy*	4th
1969	Muriel Day	The Wages of Love *by Michael Reade*	7th
1970	Dana	All Kinds Of Everything *by Derry Lindsay and Jackie Smith*	1st
1971	Angela Farrell	One Day Love *by Donald Martin and Ita Flynn*	11th
1972	Sandie Jones	Ceol an Ghrá *by Liam MacUistin and Joe Burkett*	15th
1973	Maxi	Do I Dream? *by Jack Brierly and George Crosbie*	10th
1974	Tina	Cross Your Heart *by Paul Lyttle*	7th
1975	The Swarbriggs	That's What Friends Are For *by Tommy and Jimmy Swarbrigg*	9th
1976	Red Hurley	When *by Brendan Graham*	10th

Year	Performer	Title/Writers	Place
1977	The Swarbriggs + 2 (Nicola Kerr and Alma Carroll)	It's Nice To Be In Love Again *by Tommy and Jimmy Swarbrigg*	3rd
1978	Colm T Wilkinson	Born To Sing *by Colm T Wilkinson*	5th
1979	Cathal Dunne	Happy Man *by Cathal Dunne*	5th
1980	Johnny Logan	What's Another Year? *by Shay Healy*	1st
1981	Sheeba	Horoscopes *by Joe Burkett and Jim Kelly*	5th
1982	The Duskeys	Here Today, Gone Tomorrow *by Sally Keating*	11th
1983	No Entry		
1984	Linda Martin	Terminal 3 *by Sean Sherrard (aka Johnny Logan)*	2nd
1984	Maria Christian	Wait Until The Weekend Comes *by Brendan Graham*	6th
1986	Luv Bug	You Can Count On Me *by Kevin Sheerin*	4th
1987	Johnny Logan	Hold Me Now *by Sean Sherrard (aka Johnny Logan)*	1st
1988	Jump The Gun	Take Him Home *by Peter Eades*	8th
1989	Kiev Connolly	The Real Me *by Kiev Connolly*	18th
1990	Liam Reilly	Somewhere In Europe *by Liam Reilly (of Bagatelle)*	2nd
1991	Kim Jackson	Could It Be That I'm In Love *by Liam Reilly*	10th
1992	Linda Martin	Why Me? *by Johnny Logan*	1st

Year	Performer	Title/Writers	Place
1993	Niamh Kavanagh	In Your Eyes *by Jimmy Walsh*	1st
1994	Paul Harrington and Charlie McGettigan	Rock 'n' Roll Kids *by Brendan Graham*	1st
1995	Eddie Friel	Dreamin' *by Richard Abbott and Barry Woods*	14th
1996	Eimear Quinn	The Voice *by Brendan Graham*	1st
1997	Marc Roberts	Mysterious Woman *by John Farry*	2nd
1998	Dawn Martin	It's Always Over Now *by Gerry Morgan*	9th
1999	The Mullans	When You Need Me *by Bronagh Mullan*	17th
2000	Eamonn Toal	Millennium of Love *by Gerry Simpson and Raymond Smyth*	6th
2001	Gary O'Shaughnessy	Without Your Love *by Pat Sheridan*	21st
2002	No entry		
2003	Mickey Harte	We've Got The World Tonight *by Keith Molloy and Martin Brannigan*	11th
2004	Chris Doran	If My World Stopped Turning *by Bryan McFadden and Jonathan Shorten*	23rd
2005	Donna and Joseph McCaul	Love? *by Karl Broderick* in semi final (Did not make finals)	14th
2006	Brian Kennedy	Every Song is a Cry for Love *by Brian Kennedy*	10th
2007	Dervish	They Can't Stop the Spring *by John Waters and Tommy Moran*	Last

Appendix II
Irish Bands

Band	Location	Contact/Singer
Airchords	Dublin	P Lynch
Allegros		
Altonaires	Dublin	S Young
Ambassador 7		
American Pie	Monaghan	Ronnie Griffin
Arabs		
Arrans	Arranville	
Arrivals	Cork	Declan Ryan
Arrows	Dublin	Mick Roache
Airtones		
Astronauts		
Atlantic		
Atlantis		
Avengers		
Bandits	Tuam	Tommy Ryan
Bankers		
Banshees	Belfast	Mel Austin
Barons		
Barristers	Derry	
Beaumont 7		
Bermuda	Galway	
Berwyn	Limerick	D McCormack
Big 4	Clones	Pat McGuigan
Big 8	Dublin	Brendan Bowyer
Black Aces	Kilkenny	Ollie Kearney
Black Dots	Longford	Frankie
Black Knights	Laois	B Sherman
Blue Aces	Waterford	Caroline Cheevers
Blue Angels		

Band	Location	Contact/Singer
Blue Eagles		
Boston Stompers		
Bourke Kevin	Castlebar	
Boys 'n' Girls	Galway	
Breakaways		
Bridesiders		
Broadway		
Brown Billy	Dublin	
Brown Pete	Kiltimagh	
Buckaroos	Omagh	Brian Coll
Buckshot	Dublin	Bill Ryan
Burke 7		Pat
Burmah Allstars		
Cadets	Dublin	Eileen Reid
Cadillac		
Calandos		
Campbell Pat,	Monaghan	
Candy		
Capitol	Dublin	Des Kelly
Capri		
Captains		
Carling		
Carlton		
Carnegie		
Caroline	Dublin	Earl Jordan
Carousel	Dublin	John Keating
Cascades	Gloria	
Casino	Dublin	Mel Austin
Casuals	Monaghan	Davin Knight
Cauley, Stan		
Central Seven	Athlone	
Chancellors		
Checkmates		
Chessmen	Dublin	Robert Ballagh

Band	Location	Contact/Singer
Chimes		
Clansmen		
Classic	Mullingar	
Claxton		
Clefonaires	Tubbercurry	
Cliffords		
Clipper Carlton	Strabane	Hugo Quinn
Clippertones		
Clouds		
Clubmen	Ardee	Dermot O'Brien
Coasters		
College Boys	Belfast	
College Men	Dublin	Des Smyth
Collins, Donie	Askeaton	
Columbia	Arklow	
Comet Tones		
Conquerors	Portumna	Willie Carty
Cordettes	Loughrea	
Cosmos		
Cotton Mill Boys	Dublin	Pat Maloney
Country Folk	Mullingar	Frank McCaffrey
Country Men		
Country Style		Ian Corrigan
Cousins		
Cowboys		Enda O'Riordan
Crackaways	Clara	Frank Fahy
Crescent		
Crested Knights		
Crickets		
Crowns		
Crystal Allstars	Portumna	Tom Dolphin
Cummins, Paddy		
Cyclone		
Dambusters		

Band	Location	Contact/Singer
Davitt Brothers	Wexford	
Dawnbreakers		
Dazzle Band		
Debonaires	Dublin	
Decca	Waterford	
Dee Jays		
Defenders		
Delta Allstars		
Derek Joys	Waterford	
Derry City	Derry	
Des-Etts		
Detroit		
Diamonds	Dublin	John Davitt
Diplomats		
Dixies	Cork	Brendan O'Brien
Dixielanders		Sean Lucey
Dominoes		Ballina
Drifters	Mullingar	Joe Dolan
Drumbeats	Donegal	
Dublin Corpo	Canada	Sean Fagan
Dukes	Cork	A Butler
Dunny, Jimmy	Newbridge	J Dunny
Echoes		
Eckos	Cork	D O'Keeffe
Editors	Tipperary	Kevin Flynn
Embassy	Derry	
Emperors	Derry	
Empire	Derry	
Enterprise		
Envoys	Donegal	
Epic		
Esquire	Derry	
Everglades	Monaghan	
Exciters		

Band	Location	Contact/Singer
Express	Dublin	Tony Woods
Fairways	Ballina	Gary Street
Farley, Jim	Dublin	N O'Connell
Farmers' Sons	Dublin	Liam Ryan
Fashion		
Federals		
Finnavons	Monaghan	
Finvola		
Flames		
Flamingos	Dundalk	D Keating
Fleet	Tuam	Gerry Fahy
Florida		
Flynn, Johnny	Tuam	Miko Kelly/Pat Smith
Fontana	Waterford	
Footappers	Waterford	
Freshmen	Ballymena	Derek Deane/Billy Browne
Friars		
Frielmen	Westport	
Furlong Des	Dublin	
Galway Blazers	Galway	
Gaylords	Belfast	
Gentry	Belfast	Cahir Doherty
Gents	Enniskillen	Gene Chetty
Glover Dave	North	Murial Day
Golden Star	Galway	Ray Donoghue
Graduates	Skerries	Tony Keeling
Grafton	Cookstown	Jimmy Devlin
Granada	Dublin	D Shine
Grassroots	Dublin	Tracy
Green Angels	Derry	Roy Addinel
Greenbeats	Dublin	John Keogh
Green County	Dublin	Roly Daniels
Grenadiers		
Gypsies		

Band	Location	Contact/Singer
Hanley, Jack	Tipperary	
Hanna, Fred		
Harlequins		
Harvest	Monaghan	Mary Lou
Hawaii Five-O		
Hawaiians		
Heartbeats		
High Seas		
Hi-lows	Cavan	Ian Corrigan
Hilton	Newry	Patricia O'Kelly
Hoedowners	Dublin	Sean Dunphy
Homesteaders		Gene Stewart
Hootenannys		Wee Mick
Hudson		
Hughes Denny		
Hunters		
Hurricanes		
Hustlers	Dublin	T Deegan
Huston		
Idaho		
Impact	Cork	Rory Gallagher
Immediate		
Imperial Allstars		
Imperial Imps	Dublin	
Incas		
Indians	Dublin	N Brady/E Keane
Index		
International	Manchester	Jimmy Higgins
International Allstars		
Ivory Liam	Tuam	
Jackpots		
Jets	Wicklow	Tommy Haydon
Jivenaires		
Johnson, Jimmy		

Band	Location	Contact/Singer
Jokers	Derry	
Jordan, George B	Ballina	
Jordanaires	Cavan	Gene Bannen
Kamels		
Kanaverals		
Kelly Ciaran	Athlone	
Kelly Tom	Ballina	
Kentuckians		
Kerry Blues	Tralee	DJ Curtin
Keynotes	Donegal	Charlie McCole
Killarney Jarvies		
Kings	Naas	
Ronnie Reynolds		
Klan		
Klass & Kelly		
Laganmen		
Las Vegas		
Laredo		
Leaders	Castlebar	PJ Hennelly
Lewis Walter		
Limits		
Lions	Dublin	Danny Pearse
Loughman Pat	Dublin	
Lowney Joe		
Lynch Maurice	Castlebar	
Mack Billy		
Madisons		
Mainliners	Monaghan	T McBride
Majorca	Tipperary	T Flynn
Majors	Dublin	M Mc Evoy
Maloney, Olly	Tuam	Ricky Keane
Manhattan		
Marines	Donegal	
Martells		

Band	Location	Contact/Singer
Matadors		
McCafferty, P		
McCafferty, L		
McFarland, B	Ballymena	
McIntyre, Gay	Derry	
Melochords		
Melody Aces	Tyrone	
Melody Makers		
Melotones		
Memories	Dublin	Mike Swan
Memphis		R Daniels
Merry Minstrels		
Mexicans	Bray	A Cranny
Miami	Dublin	Dickie Rock
Mighty Avons	Cavan	J Smith
Millionaires	Dublin	J Doherty
Monarchs	Limerick	Tommy Drennan
Moonglows		
Montrose		
Mulcahy M	Mitchelstown	
Music Box	Dublin	
Mystics	Roscommon	
Navak	Cavan	S McCormack
Nevada	Dublin	T Hayden
Newport, Kim	Ballina	T Kelly
Niagra	Ballyhaunis	J Conway
Night Squad		
Nomads	Kilkenny	T Cantwell
Northern Comets		
O'Callaghan, M	Buttevent	E Nedwell
Oceans		
Odeon	Tipperary	
Ohio	Tuam	G Cronin
Oriole	Shrule	E Heneghan

Band	Location	Contact/Singer
Pacific	Dublin	Sean Fagan
Paladin		
Palms		
Paragon Seven	Dundalk	G Cahill
Paramount	Tuam	K Eagleton
Partners		
Pasadena		
Philosophers	Galway	D Ward
Pirates	Limerick	
Platters	Omagh	Rob Strong
Playboys	Donegal	
Playmates	Donegal	
Polka Dots	Omagh	Frankie McBride
Power Pack		
Premier Aces	Roscommon	P Malone
Presidents		
Pressmen		
Problems	Tuam	F Carroll
Quartermasters		
Quigley, J	Derry	
Radiant		
Radio	Dublin	L Ryan
Ramblers		
Raindrops	Galway	C Grace
Ravens		
Raydots		
Real McCoy	Dublin	M O'Brien
Red Admirals		
Red Seven		
Regal	Cork	D Ryan
Regency		
Rhythm Boys	Roscommon	Treacy
Rhythm Stars		
Ripcords		

Band	Location	Contact/Singer
Rising Son		
Riviera	Ballyhaunis	S Cribben
Rocky Mountain Seven	Ballindine	M Donoghue
Royal	Waterford	Brendan Bowyer
Royal Aces		
Royal Blues	Claremorris	D Carroll
Royal Chords	Castlebar	K Bourke
Royal Earls	Dublin	S Jones
Royal Safari		
Ruane Jack	Ballina	
Rumble Band		T Palmer
Safari		
Sahara		P Hanrahan
Sands		T Kenny
Santa Fe	Strabane	
Savannah		
Savoy	Waterford	
Seasons		
Secrets		
Senators		
Shine Brendan		
Silhouettes	Belfast	
Silver Pennies		
Skyrockets	Enniskillen	C Kettles
Slieve Foy	Donegal	
Slick Six	Kerry	
Snowdrifters		
Sounds		
Squires		
Stage Two	Cork	J McCarthy
Stellas		
Sterling		
Strands		
Sturrock Jimmy		

Band	Location	Contact/Singer
Sundowners		
Swallows	Galway	C Murphy
Swinging Viscounts		
Swingtime Aces	Athenry	J Reilly
Tara		
Tartans		
Teenbeats	Dublin	Betty Anne
Teeveetones	Cavan	S McCormack
Telstars		
Tides	Galway	T Small
Tigermen		
Times	Mullingar	Tommy and Jimmy Swarbrigg
Top Seven		F Chism
Top League	Limerick	Tommy Drennan
Tourists		
Traynor, H	Armagh	
Trend		
Trenniers	Enniskillen	
Trixons	Longford	
Tropical		
Troubado		
U-Kons		
Valentine		
Vanguard Six	Tralee	T Callaghan
Vards		
Ventures	Monaghan	T Hughes
Vocards		
Victors		
Vienna		
Vikings	Dundalk	P O'Hare
Viscounts		P Russell
Visions		
Voxenaires	Kilkenny	J Grace

Band	Location	Contact/Singer
Walsh, Brose	Castlebar	
Warriors		
West Coasters	Galway	
Western All-stars	Galway	
Witness		Colm Wilkinson
Woodpeckers	Dundalk	
Woods, K	Drumshambo	
Yaks		
Young Shadows	Dublin	
Zodiacs		
Zulus		Paddy Blanche

Appendix III
Where Are They Now?

Peter Bardon (Greenbeats, Tina and Real McCoy)	Publishing
Don Lydon (Philosophers)	Politics
Donie Cassidy (Jim Tobin and Firehouse)	Politics/Recording
Albert Reynolds (Promoter)	Politics
Robert Ballagh (Chessmen)	Graphic Artist
Fergie Gibson (D O'Brien)	Astrology
Ronan Collins (Dickie Rock)	Radio
Maxi (Music Box)	Radio
Hugo Duncan (Ulster)	Radio
Johnny Anderson (Ulster)	Radio
Jimmy Greally (Movement)	Radio
Derek Davis (Tree Tops)	RTÉ
Sam Smyth (Spotlight)	Journalist
Tony Keeling (Graduates)	Teaching
Pat Lynch (Airchords)	Teaching
Pat McCabe (Oklahoma)	Writer/Films
Sean Fagan (Pacific)	Canada
Brendan Bowyer (Royal)	USA/Ireland
Dickie Rock (Miami)	Dublin
Colm Connolly (Paramount)	Journalist/Cyprus
Joe Dolan (Drifters)	Mullingar
Larry Cunningham (Mighty Avons)	Granard
Twink (Adele King) (Big 8)	TV/Theatre
Eileen Reid (Cadets)	TV/Theatre
Seán Fennessey (J Farley)	RTÉ
Tommy Swarbrigg (Drifters/Times)	Promoter
Jim Aiken (Slane/Vicar Street)	Promoter (died 2007